100
Weekend
Cross-Stitch Gifts

by Barbara Finwall
and Nancy Javier

BANAR DESIGNS, Inc.

Meredith® Press
New York, New York

Dear Crafter,

Gift-giving is a heart-warming gesture, especially when the gift is hand-crafted. Within these pages you'll find 100 delightful gifts to share with family and friends. Some you'll want to make again as a treat for yourself.

This charming collection of gifts-to-be boasts something for any occasion—Valentine's Day, Mother's Day, Father's Day, birthdays, anniversaries, Christmas, decorations for the home, and things to wear.

The directions for each are divided into three easy-to-follow steps: Gather the materials, cross-stitch, then add any finishing details. Each point is clearly explained and each gift attractively photographed.

We at Meredith® Press strive to bring you the highest quality craft books, full of exciting designs, innovative uses for projects, easy-to-read instructions and charts, and full color photographs. We are proud to bring you *100 Weekend Cross-Stitch Gifts,* and hope you will enjoy using it to create many treasured gifts.

Sincerely,

Jennifer Darling

Jennifer Darling
Editorial Project Manager

For BANAR DESIGNS, Inc.:
BANAR DESIGNS, Inc. Principles: Barbara Finwall, Nancy Javier, Arleen Bennett
Design Directors: Barbara Finwall and Nancy Javier
Editorial Director: Jan Mollet Evans, MORE THAN WORDS
Designers: Barbara Finwall, Holly Witt, Melissa Secola, Vicky Dye, Nancy Javier, Pat Van Note
Computer Graphics: Amparo Orozco, Wade Rollins, Holly Witt
Chart Coordinator: Amparo Orozco
Stitch Coordinators: Marita Dionisio and Nemie Torres
Stitchers: Nemie Torres, Marita Dionisio, Yoshiko Lehmann, Hatsue Honey, Kathryn Lee, Arleen Bennett, Betsy Gleason
Seamstress and Finisher: Patsy Needham
Proofreaders: Marita Dionisio, Nemie Torres, Joan Arnold, Holly Witt, Nancy Javier
Staff: Yoshiko Ball, Tamiyo Dye, Cecil Ekrut, Jean Jarrell, Danny LaPointe, Mateo Nicolas, Liz Opean, Ayako Secola, Margarita White, Leticia Zapata

Framed photographs in project photos courtesy of William Ahrend Photography, Fallbrook, California

Meredith® Press is an imprint of Meredith® Books:
President, Book Group: Joseph J. Ward
Vice-President, Editorial Director: Elizabeth P. Rice

For Meredith® Press:
Executive Editor: Connie Schrader
Editorial Project Manager: Jennifer Darling
Assistant Art Director: Tom Wegner
Copy Editor: Jennifer Speer Ramundt
Photographer: Scott Little
Cover Photographer: Perry Struse
Production Manager: Bill Rose

ISBN: 0-696-02386-5
Library of Congress Catalog Number: 92-085380

Printed in the United States of America
10 9 8 7 6 5 4

All of us at Meredith® Press are dedicated to offering you, our customer, the best books we can create. We are particularly concerned that all of our instructions for making projects are clear and accurate. Please address your correspondence to: Customer Service Department, Meredith® Press, Meredith Corporation, 150 East 52nd Street, New York, NY 10022.

If you would like to order additional copies of any of our books, call 1-800-678-2803 or check with your local bookstore.

Introduction

In our busy world, the demands of home, family, and work seem to make the days just fly by. We barely have time to take a short breather on the weekend and another activity-filled week is upon us. Sometimes it seems we don't have time to show those closest to us how much we care.

With precisely those thoughts in mind, we created *100 Weekend Cross-Stitch Gifts*, a compendium of easy-to-do projects that can be made in just one weekend. Each project is intended to be your gift to someone special—a gift that will be appreciated and treasured by the person receiving it because it was lovingly handmade by you.

We hope that this book will become a handy reference guide in your library—a source to be used again and again for last minute gifts that look as if you worked on them for weeks rather than hours.

Every project is as easy as one, two, three:

1. Gather materials: Start with this step on Friday evening. We've kept the materials simple, with very few specialty products; we even give you alternate methods in case you can't find those products.

2. Stitch: Use your Saturday and Sunday hours as your schedule allows. Cross-stitching is relaxing and easy to do, even while you watch your favorite TV program.

3. Finish: Put the finishing touches on your gift Sunday afternoon or evening. Many projects actually require no finishing; others use simple techniques that yield elegant results.

In no time at all, you'll find you've cross-stitched and finished a unique gift that's ready to be presented to that special person. Each person who receives a handmade gift will cherish your thoughtfulness and marvel at the time it must have taken you to craft such a treasure. Little will they know you made it in just one weekend!

Introduction

Gifts of Love

Gifts for Special Occasions

Gifts for Holidays

Gifts for the Home

Gifts to Wear

Gifts of Love

❖ ❖ ❖

Brighten someone's day with a cheery

remembrance to cherish for years to come.

A floral photo album for mom,

a handsome fishing cap for grandpa,

or a sweet pastel baby blanket are among

the treasures that await.

A Rose Garden

For Mom

Family Photo Album,
page 8

Family Photo Frame,
page 8

Sachet,
page 12

Family Photo Album

1. Gather Materials

Aida fabric: 14 count, white, 6 inches square
Photo album: Ring-binder type, approximately 11x12 inches
Cardboard: Heavyweight, 12 inches square
Poster Board: Lightweight, 11x24 inches
Batting: 1 inch thick, ⅓ yard, 45 inches wide
Fabric: Blue and white stripe, ¾ yard (45 inches wide); solid blue, 8 inches square
Gathered eyelet lace: White, 1 inch x 3½ yards
Rattail cord: Light blue, 3½ yards
Feather-edged satin ribbon: Light blue, ⅜ inch x 2½ yards; pink, ¼ inch x 1¾ yards
Ribbon roses: Pink with green leaves, ½ inch wide, 3
Thick, white glue and/or glue gun
Scissors
Tapestry needle

2. Stitch

Follow the cross-stitching instructions given in Cross-Stitch Basics.

3. Finish

Finishing instructions for covering photo albums and padded shapes are given in General Project Instructions. The following are additional instructions for this album.
■ Cover the album with the striped fabric.
■ Glue eyelet lace on the inside of the covers and spine, extending it out about ¾ inch.
■ Glue rattail cord around all edges on the outside where the cover meets the lace.
■ Cut a small and large heart from batting and cardboard (see patterns above).
■ Cover large heart with batting and blue fabric.

■ Glue eyelet lace to back of large heart, starting at the V at top of the heart; extend it out about ¾ inch.
■ Glue rattail cord around the outside of the large heart where the lace meets the fabric, starting and ending at the V at top of the heart.
■ Cover small heart with batting and cross-stitched fabric. Glue eyelet lace and rattail cord around edge, as you did on the large heart, starting at the V on top of the heart.
■ Glue small heart in center of large heart, and glue large heart in center of album front cover.
■ Tie a triple-loop bow with the feather-edged ribbon (loops 1½ inches, 2¼ inches, and 3 inches wide. Glue it to the center top of the album cover, twisting the tails of the bow and gluing them to the album as shown in the photo.
■ Glue the three ribbon roses to the center of the bow.

Family Photo Album
Full-Size Patterns

Family Photo Frame

1. Gather Materials

Aida fabric: 14 count, white, 8 inches square
Photo frame: 5¼ inches square with heart cutout *or* heavyweight cardboard 5¼x12 inches (patterns on page 10)
Fabric: Coordinating plain or print cotton or cotton blend to cover the frame backing and easel, 12 inches square
Batting: 5¼ inches square
Gathered eyelet lace: White, 1x24 inches
Rattail cord: Light blue, 38 inches
Thick, white glue and/or glue gun
Scissors
Tapestry needle

2. Stitch

Follow the cross-stitching instructions given in Cross-Stitch Basics.

Family Photo Album Chart

Stitch Count: 44 x 33

3. Finish

Finishing instructions for covering photo frames are given in General Project Instructions. The following are additional instructions for this frame.

■ Cover the photo frame with the cross-stitched Aida fabric.
■ Glue eyelet lace on the back of the frame, extending it out about ¾ inch, before assembling front and back of frame.
■ Glue rattail cord around all edges on the front where the cross-stitched fabric meets the lace.

(continued)

Floss: (Symbol indicates color on chart.)

Symbol	Color name	DMC #	Anchor #
•	Light pink	818	49
○	Medium pink	3733	76
●	Dark pink*	3731	77
V	Light blue	932	920
▽	Medium blue	931	921
▼	Dark blue	930	922
/	Light green	912	205
◢	Dark green	910	229
	Black*	310	403

*Backstitch lettering with two strands of dark pink and bow with one strand of black.

Photo Frame
(continued)

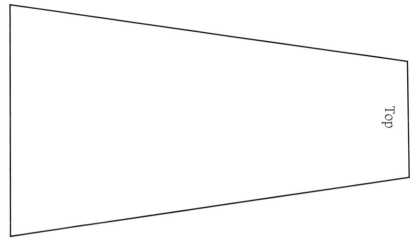

Family Photo Frame Stand
Full-Size Pattern

Floss: (Symbol indicates color on chart.)

Symbol	Color name	DMC #	Anchor #
·	Light pink	818	49
○	Medium pink	224	894
●	Dark pink	3731	77
V	Light blue	932	920
▽	Medium blue	931	921
▼	Dark blue	930	922
/	Light green	912	205
◢	Dark green	910	229
	Black*	310	403

*Backstitch bow with one strand of black.

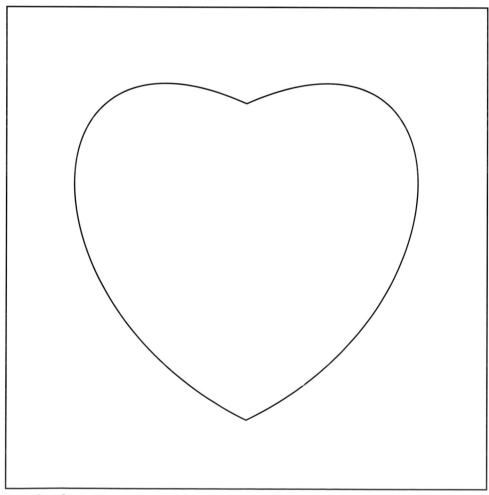

Family Photo Frame
Full-Size Pattern

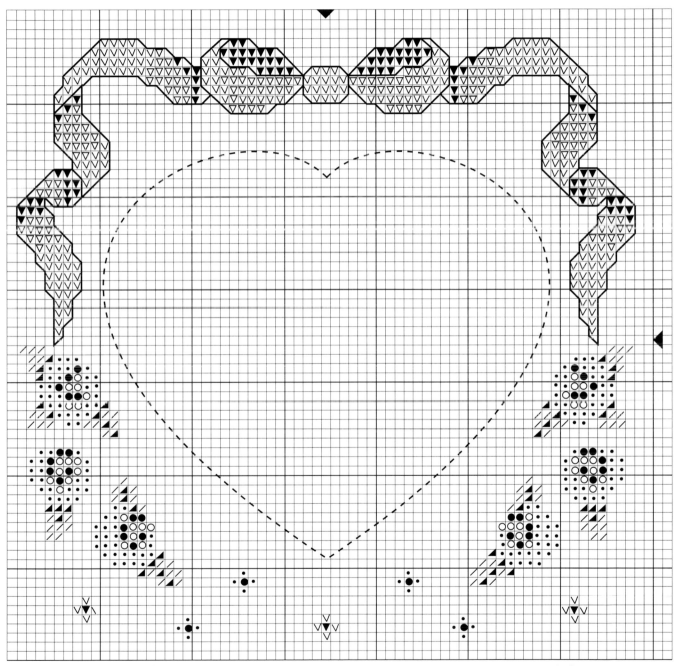

Family Photo Frame Chart

Stitch Count: 67 x 65

Sachet

1. Gather Materials

Aida fabric: 14 count, white, 5½x12 inches

Satin lining fabric: Pink, 3½x10 inches

Feather-edged ribbon: ¼x16 inches

Ribbon rose: Pink with leaves, ½ inch

Lace: White, ¾x7 inches

Potpourri: About ¾ cup

Sewing machine (optional)

Sewing needle and white thread

Scissors

Tapestry needle

Iron

2. Stitch

Fold the Aida fabric in half to form a 5½x6-inch rectangle; press the fold with an iron to crease it. Unfold the fabric, and cross-stitch the design in the center of the upper half of the fabric (with the raw edge at the top and the fold at the bottom). Follow the cross-stitching instructions given in Cross-Stitch Basics.

3. Finish

■ After cross-stitching the design on Aida, cut off 1 inch of the fabric on all four sides, leaving a 3½x10-inch piece of cross-stitched fabric.

■ Fold cross-stitched Aida fabric in half along the pressed fold with the stitching inside. Stitch ¼-inch seams on each side; leave the top open.

■ Turn the bag right side out. Fold the top (open) edge into the bag ½ inch, and press with an iron to crease it.

■ Stitch the lace ¼ inch inside the folded edge of the bag, extending ½ inch of lace above the bag. Lay aside.

■ Fold the satin lining fabric in half, dull side out, to form a 3½x5-inch rectangle. Press fold to crease. Stitch ¼-inch seams on each side. Do not turn the lining bag right side out.

■ Fold the top (raw) edge of the satin lining bag down to the outside of the bag ½ inch, and press with an iron to crease it.

■ Place the lining bag inside the Aida bag, pushing it down so the creased top edge of the lining is just inside the creased top edge of the Aida bag; be sure the lace still extends above both bags about ½ inch. Whipstitch the creased edges of the Aida and lining bags together with a needle and thread.

■ Fill sachet with potpourri.

■ Tie feather-edged ribbon tightly around top of bag in a bow, about 1 inch from the open edge, to close the bag. Trim ends of the ribbon at an angle; attach ribbon rose to center of bow (see photo, page 7).

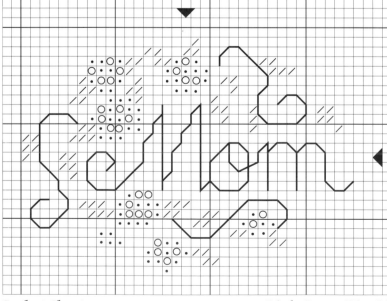

Sachet Chart Stitch Count: 35 x 25

Floss: (Symbol indicates color on chart.)

Symbol	Color name	DMC #	Anchor #
•	Light pink	818	49
○	Medium pink*	3731	77
╱	Light green	912	205
	Dark green*	319	218

*Backstitch stems with one strand of dark green. Backstitch letters with two strands of medium pink.

Fair and Square

For Dad

Dad's Photo Frame,
page 14

Coffee Mug,
page 16

FOR
DAD'S
BOOKS

Bookmark,
page 14

Bookmark

1. Gather Materials

Aida fabric: 14 count, black, 6x8½ inches
Thick, white glue
Scissors
Tapestry needle
Iron

2. Stitch

Follow the cross-stitching instructions given in Cross-Stitch Basics.

3. Finish

■ After cross-stitching the design on Aida, cut off 1 inch of the fabric on all four sides, leaving a 4x6½-inch piece of stitched fabric.
■ Fringe the top and bottom ½ inch by pulling out the horizontal threads.
■ Fold back the fabric on either side of the design until the sides meet in the center of the back. Press the folds with the iron to crease. The bookmark should now be 2 inches wide and 6½ inches high, including fringe.
■ Unfold the fabric, and apply an even coat of glue to the back of each flap; smooth flaps firmly back into place and allow to dry. As an alternative to gluing, you can stitch the flaps together in the center back of the bookmark.

Dad's Photo Frame

1. Gather materials

Aida fabric: 14 count, black, 6 inches square

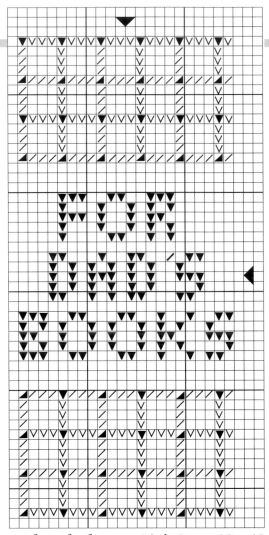

Bookmark Chart   Stitch Count: 22 x 49

Floss: (Symbol indicates color on chart.)

Symbol	Color name	DMC #	Anchor #
V	Light blue	322	146
▼	Dark blue	311	148
/	Light green	912	205
◢	Dark green	319	318

Photo frame: 3⅜x4⅛ inches with oval cutout *or* heavyweight cardboard, 4⅛x10 inches (patterns on page 15)
Fabric: Coordinating plain or print cotton or cotton/polyester blend to cover frame backing and easel
Batting: 3⅜x4⅛ inches
Rattail cord: Royal blue, 16 inches
Thick, white glue and/or glue gun
Scissors
Tapestry needle

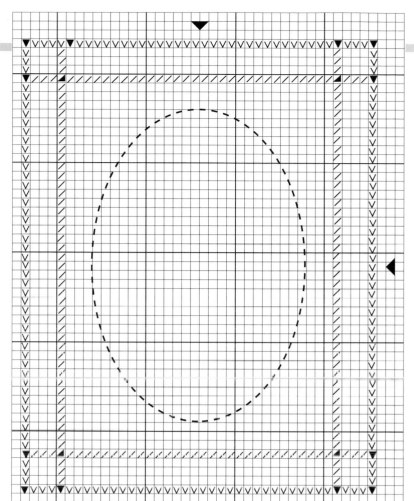

Dad's Photo Frame Chart   Stitch Count: 40 x 51

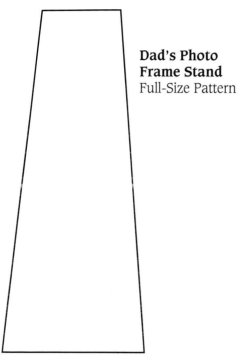

**Dad's Photo
Frame Stand**
Full-Size Pattern

2. Stitch

Follow the cross-stitching instructions given in Cross-Stitch Basics.

3. Finish

Finishing instructions for covering photo frames are given in General Project Instructions. The following are additional instructions for this frame.

■ Cover the photo frame with the cross-stitched Aida fabric, trimming off excess fabric.

■ Glue rattail cord around edges before assembling front and back of frame.

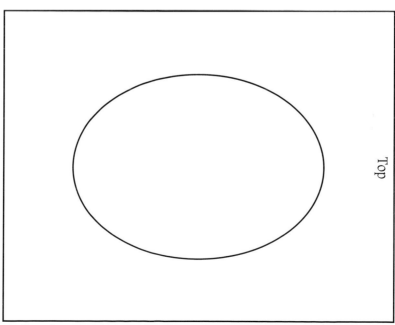

Top

Dad's Photo Frame
Full-Size Pattern

Coffee Mug

1. Gather Materials

Aida fabric: 14 count, black, 6¼x13½ inches
Plastic mug: Two-part, to allow fabric insert, (Fun Mugs® from Kelly's Crafts, Inc.)
Thick, white glue
Scissors
Tapestry needle
Iron

2. Stitch

Follow the cross-stitching instructions given in Cross-Stitch Basics.

Floss: (Symbol indicates color on chart.)

Symbol	Color name	DMC #	Anchor #
V	Light blue*	798	137
▼	Dark blue	311	148
/	Light green	912	205
◢	Dark green	319	218
	*Backstitch with two strands of light blue.		

3. Finish

■ After cross-stitching the design on Aida, cut off 1 inch of the fabric on all four sides, leaving a 4¼x11½-inch piece of stitched fabric.
■ Fold back the fabric ½ inch on all four sides of the design. Press the folds with the iron to crease.
■ Trim excess fabric away at the corners, cutting at a 45-degree angle.
■ Unfold the fabric, and apply an even coat of glue to the back of each flap; smooth flaps firmly back into place and allow to dry. As an alternative to gluing, you can stitch the flaps down.
■ Separate the inner and outer layers of the cup by putting your thumb on the outside and your fingers on the inside, and pushing down with your thumb while pulling up with your fingers.
■ Place the cross-stitched Aida fabric just inside the clear, outer layer of the mug, overlapping the ends of the fabric at the handle. Note: Because of the angled shape of the mug, the ends will not overlap evenly, but rather at an angle.
■ Replace the inner, white liner of the mug, snapping it in place firmly.

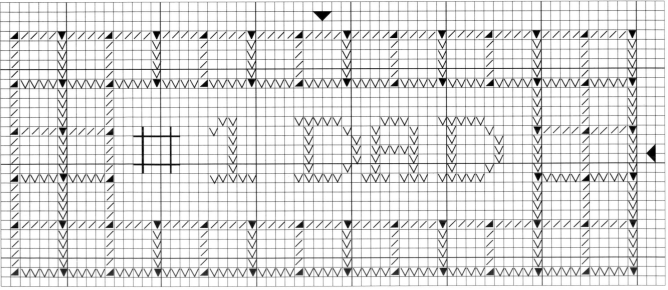

Coffee Mug Chart

Stitch Count: 66 x 26

A Place for Everything

Key Case,
page 19

Keys

MY BRAG BOOK

Brag Book,
page 18

Scissors

Scissors Case,
page 20

Brag Book

1. Gather Materials

Aida fabric: 14 count, white, 4x6 inches
Photo album: Approximately 4½x5½ inches
Cardboard: Heavyweight, 3x4 inches
Poster board: Lightweight, 6x8 inches
Batting: 1 inch thick, 5½x15 inches
Fabric: Dark background with pink and green floral pattern, ¼ yard
Gathered eyelet lace: White, 1x30 inches
Rattail cord: Pink, 45 inches; forest green, 84 inches
Satin ribbon: Pink, ⅜x30 inches; forest green, ⅛x96 inches
Thick, white glue and/or glue gun
Scissors
Tapestry needle

2. Stitch

Follow the cross-stitching instructions given in Cross-Stitch Basics.

3. Finish

Finishing instructions for covering photo albums and padded shapes are given in General Project Instructions. The following are additional instructions for this album.

■ Cover the album with the floral fabric. Before you glue in the inner linings, cut 15-inch lengths of satin ribbon (two pink and six green); glue the ends of one pink and three green ribbons inside the center edge of each of the album covers to act as ties. Cover the glued ribbon ends with the fabric lining.

■ Glue eyelet lace on the inside of the covers and spine, extending it out about ¾ inch.

■ Take 45-inch lengths of the pink and the green rattail cord. As you twist the two cords together, glue them down where the floral fabric meets the eyelet lace at the edges of the album.

■ Cut a 3x4-inch rectangle from batting and from cardboard. Cover cardboard rectangle with the batting, then the cross-stitched Aida fabric.

■ Glue a double row of green rattail cord around the stitched rectangle where the Aida fabric meets the album.

■ Glue rectangle in center of album front.

■ Tie the pink and green ribbons in a bow to close the album. Cut ends of ribbons at an angle.

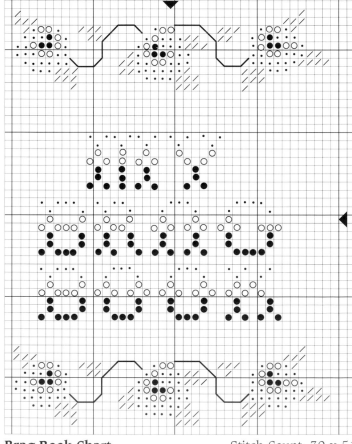

Brag Book Chart   Stitch Count: 39 x 51

Floss: (Symbol indicates color on chart.)

Symbol	Color name	DMC #	Anchor #
•	Light pink	776	74
○	Medium pink	957	75
●	Dark pink	956	54
╱	Medium green	912	205
	Dark green*	910	230

*Backstitch stems with one strand of dark green.

Key Case

1. Gather Materials

Key case: Premade with even-weave fabric band sewn in (Adam Originals) *or* 3x4-inch key case without even-weave band and the following materials:
> **Aida fabric:** 14 count, ecru, 6½x4½ inches, *or* Ribband: 6½x1½ inches with lace or scalloped edge
> **Lace:** Ecru, ½x12 inches (if using plain Aida)
> **Washable fabric glue**
> **Needle and white sewing thread (optional)**

Scissors
Tapestry needle

2. Stitch

One edge of the Aida fabric is not stitched to the key case on the premade version. Place your fingers and needle between the Aida and floral fabrics and cross-stitch. Follow the cross-stitching instructions given in Cross-Stitch Basics.

If you cannot locate a key case premade with an even-weave band, cross-stitch the design on a strip of Aida fabric wide enough to go across the case plus 3 inches or on Ribband and finish according to the following instructions.

3. Finish

Note: The key case requires no finishing. However, you may wish to whipstitch or glue the edge of the Aida fabric to the floral fabric beneath it when the cross-stitching is complete. If adding a band of cross-stitching to a purchased or home-sewn key case, follow the instructions below.

■ After cross-stitching the design on Aida, cut off 1 inch of the fabric from all four sides, leaving a 4½x3½-inch piece of stitched fabric. If using Ribband, cut 1 inch off only the ends.

■ Fold back the Aida fabric ½ inch on all four sides of the stitched design. Press the folds with an iron to crease. If using Ribband, fold back only the ends and press.

■ Trim excess Aida fabric away at the corners, cutting at a 45-degree angle.

■ Unfold the fabric, and apply an even coat of glue to each flap; smooth the flaps firmly into place and allow to dry. As an alternative to gluing, you can stitch the flaps down.

■ Apply fabric glue to the entire back of the stitched piece of Aida or Ribband; center on the key case and press in place (pin down until glue dries, if necessary). As an alternative to gluing the cross-stitched piece, you can sew it to the key case with a needle and thread.

■ Glue or sew lace around the edge of the Aida strip (see photo, page 17).

Floss: (Symbol indicates color on chart.)

Symbol	Color name	DMC #	Anchor #
•	Light pink	3733	76
●	Dark pink	956	42
/	Light green	955	203
	Dark green*	910	229
V	Light blue	932	920
	Black*	310	403

*Backstitch the stems with one strand of dark green and the lettering with two strands of black.

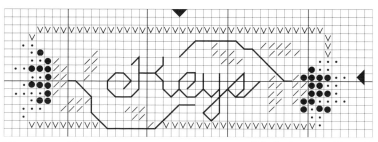

Key Case Chart   Stitch Count: 40 x 13

Scissors Case

1. Gather Materials

Scissors case: Premade with even-weave fabric band sewn in (Adam Originals) *or* 3x5-inch scissors case without even-weave band and the following materials:
  Aida fabric: 14 count, ecru, 6x4½ inches, *or* Ribband: 5x1½ inches with lace or scalloped edge
  Lace: Ecru, ½x12 inches (if using plain Aida)
  Washable fabric glue
  Needle and white sewing thread (optional)
Scissors
Tapestry needle

2. Stitch

One edge of the Aida fabric is not stitched to the scissors case on the premade version. Place your fingers and needle between the Aida and floral fabrics and cross-stitch. Follow the cross-stitching instructions given in Cross-Stitch Basics.

If you cannot locate a scissors case premade with an even-weave band, cross-stitch the design on a strip of Aida fabric wide enough to go across the case plus 3 inches or on Ribband and finish according to the following instructions.

3. Finish

Note: The scissors case premade with an even-weave band requires no finishing. However, you may wish to whipstitch or glue the edge of the Aida fabric to the floral fabric beneath it when the cross-stitching is complete.

If adding a band of cross-stitching to a purchased scissors case, follow the instructions below.

■ After cross-stitching the design on Aida, cut off 1 inch of the fabric from all four sides, leaving a 4x3½-inch piece of stitched fabric. If using Ribband, cut 1 inch off only the ends.

■ Fold back of the Aida fabric ½ inch on all four sides of the cross-stitched design. Press the folds with an iron to crease. If using Ribband, fold back only the ends and press.

■ Trim excess Aida fabric away at the corners, cutting at a 45-degree angle.

■ Unfold the fabric, and apply an even coating of glue to each flap; smooth the flaps firmly into place and allow to dry.

■ Apply fabric glue to the entire back of the cross-stitched piece of Aida or Ribband; center on the scissors case and press in place (pin down until glue dries, if necessary). As an alternative to gluing the cross-stitched piece, you can sew it to the scissors case with a needle and thread.

■ Glue or sew lace around the edge of the Aida strip (see photo, page 17).

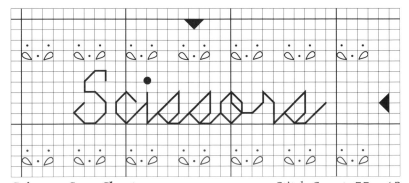

Scissors Case Chart   Stitch Count: 33 x 12

Floss: (Symbol indicates color on chart.)

Symbol	Color name	DMC #	Anchor #
•	Light pink	3733	76
⟂	Green lazy daisy*	955	203
	Black*	310	403

*Backstitch the letters with two strands of black. Use two strands of green and lazy daisy stitches for the leaves.

Good Sport

Fishing Cap,
page 22

Towel,
page 23

Fishing Cap

1. Gather Materials

Hat: Premade with even-weave fabric sewn in (Crafter's Pride, No. 10660), *or* plain hat without even-weave band and the following materials:

Aida fabric: 14 count, white, 6x7 inches
Washable fabric glue
Iron
Scissors
Tapestry needle

2. Stitch

Fold down the protective panel inside the front of the premade hat to gain access to the Aida fabric. Cross-stitch the design, and replace the protective panel. Follow the cross-stitching instructions given in Cross-Stitch Basics.

If you cannot locate a hat premade with an even-weave insert, cross-stitch the design on Aida fabric and finish according to the following instructions.

3. Finish

Note: The hat premade with an even-weave insert requires no finishing. If adding a cross-stitched panel to a plain hat, follow the instructions below.

■ After cross-stitching the design on Aida, cut off 1 inch of the fabric from all four sides, leaving a 4x5-inch piece of cross-stitched fabric.

■ Fold back the Aida fabric ½ inch on all four sides of the cross-stitched design. Press the folds with an iron to crease.

■ Trim excess fabric away at the corners, cutting at a 45-degree angle.

■ Unfold the fabric, and apply an even coat of glue to each flap; smooth the flaps firmly into place and allow to dry.

■ Apply fabric glue to the entire back of the stitched piece of Aida; center it on the front of the hat and press in place (pin down until glue dries, if necessary). As an alternative to gluing the stitched piece, you can sew it to the hat.

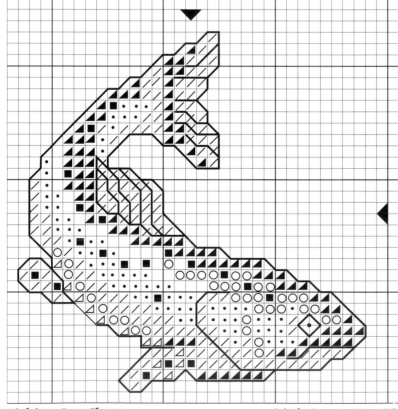

Fishing Cap Chart   Stitch Count: 31 x 32

Floss: (Symbol indicates color on chart.)

Symbol	Color name	DMC #	Anchor #
/	Light green	472	264
◿	Medium green	470	267
◢	Dark green	936	269
○	Yellow	743	302
•	Medium pink	899	55
■	Black*	310	403

*Back-stitch with one strand of black, eye is a French knot done in black.

Towel

1. Gather Materials

Towel: Premade, 14x28 inches, with even-weave fabric insert woven in vertically (Charles Craft, #TT1600-6221), *or* plain towel without even-weave band and the following materials:

    Aida fabric: 14 count, white, 7x31 inches, *or* Ribband: 2½x31 inches

    Washable ribbon: Medium blue, ¼x60 inches (if not using Ribband)

    Iron

    Sewing machine or needle and thread

Scissors

Tapestry needle

2. Stitch

Cross-stitch the design on the band of the premade towel, choosing the ball design desired (see alternate ball charts, page 24). Follow the cross-stitching instructions given in Cross-Stitch Basics.

If you cannot locate a towel premade with an even-weave insert, cross-stitch the design on Aida or on Ribband and finish according to the following instructions.

3. Finish

Note: The towel premade with an even-weave insert requires no finishing.

(continued)

Floss: (Symbol indicates color on chart.)

Symbol	Color name	DMC #	Anchor #
V	Blue	798	146
L	Purple	554	108
/	Green	910	229
○	Red	321	47
—	Gray	415	398
	Black*	310	403

*Backstitch with one strand of black.

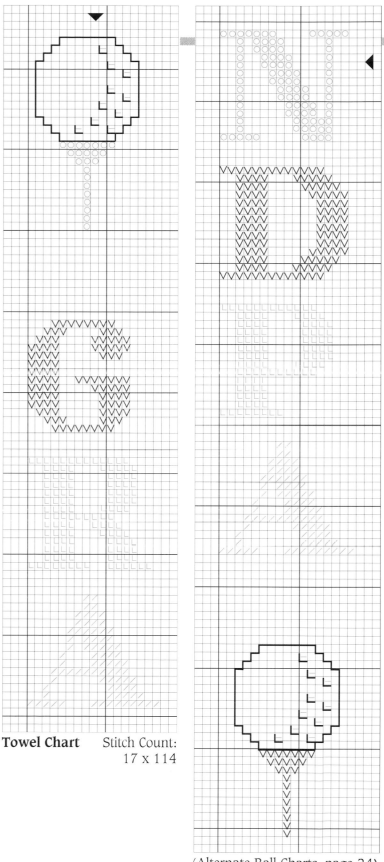

Towel Chart   Stitch Count: 17 x 114

(Alternate Ball Charts, page 24)

Towel
(continued)

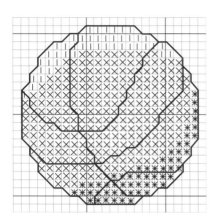

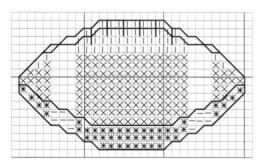

If adding a cross-stitched panel to a plain towel, follow the instructions below. Measurements assume the towel is 14x28 inches; adjust as necessary.

■ After cross-stitching the design on Aida, cut off 1 inch of the fabric from all four sides, leaving a 5x29-inch piece of cross-stitched fabric. If using Ribband, cut 1 inch off on only the ends.

■ Fold back the Aida fabric ½ inch on all four sides of the cross-stitched design. Press the folds with an iron to crease. If using Ribband, fold back only the ends and press.

■ Trim excess Aida fabric away at the corners, cutting at a 45-degree angle.

■ Stitch the flaps down.

■ Cut the washable ribbon in half. Sew a piece along each of the long edges of the Aida with half on the fabric and half off; fold ½ inch to the back of the fabric on each end.

■ Center the cross-stitched piece on the towel and sew in place.

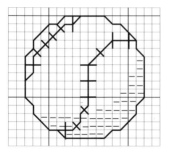

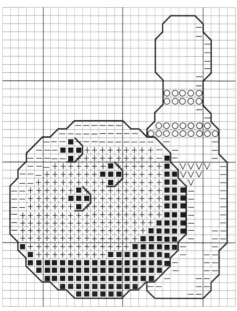

Alternate Ball Charts

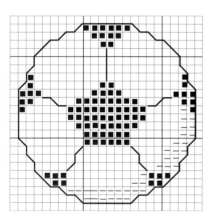

Floss: (Symbol indicates color on chart.)

Symbol	Color name	DMC #	Anchor #
V	Blue	798	146
L	Purple	554	108
/	Green	910	229
○	Red	321	47
—	Gray	415	398
	Black*	310	403

*Backstitch with one strand of black.

Just Ducky

Bib,
page 27

Heart-Shaped Pillow,
page 28

molly

Birth Sampler,
page 26

BORN THIS DAY
MEGAN HILL
9/21/92

Receiving Blanket,
page 29

Birth Sampler

1. Gather Materials

Aida fabric: 14 count, white, 7x9 inches
Satin ribbon: Pink, ⅜x24 inches
Wooden dowel: ¼ x4½ inches
Thick, white glue
Tapestry needle
Scissors
Iron

2. Stitch

Follow the cross-stitching and personalizing instructions given in Cross-Stitch Basics and Alphabets for Personalizing. Choose letters for personalizing from the alphabet chart on page 169.

3. Finish

■ Cut 1 inch off all edges of the fabric to form a 5x7-inch rectangle.
■ Fringe the bottom ½ inch of the fabric by pulling out the horizontal threads.
■ Fold back the fabric ½ inch on each side of the design; press with an iron to crease.
■ Unfold the fabric, and apply an even coat of glue to each flap; smooth flaps firmly back into place and allow to dry. As an alternative to gluing, you can stitch the flaps down.
■ Lay the satin ribbon along the dowel with approximately 10 inches extending beyond the dowel on each end.
■ Wrap 1 inch of the top of the Aida fabric over the ribbon and dowel to form a casing; glue or stitch in place. Allow glue to dry.
■ Bring the ends of the pink ribbon up about 2 inches above the dowel and tie in a loose bow. Cut off excess ribbon, leaving about 3-inch ends on each side.

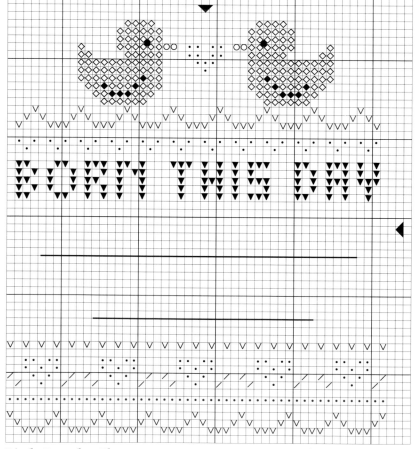

Birth Sampler Chart   Stitch Count: 49 x 53

Floss: (Symbol indicates color on chart.)

Symbol	Color name	DMC #	Anchor #
◇	Medium yellow	743	302
◆	Dark yellow	783	306
V	Medium blue	813	160
▼	Dark blue*	825	162
·	Medium pink	957	52
	Dark pink*	956	42
○	Orange	722	323
/	Light green	703	238
	Black*	310	403

*Backstitch slashes in date with dark blue. Eyes are French knots done in black. Personalize with dark pink.

Bib

1. Gather Materials

Borderline Bib: White/banana ice, premade with 14-count Aida insert, 2x10 inches (Charles Craft, BB-6659), *or* premade bib and the following materials:

> **Aida fabric:** 14 count, white, 4x13 inches, *or* Ribband: 2x13 inches, with scalloped edge
>
> **Washable ribbon or lace:** ¼x21 inches
>
> **Iron**
>
> **Sewing Machine or needle and thread**

Tapestry needle
Scissors

Floss: (Symbol indicates color on chart.)

Symbol	Color name	DMC #	Anchor #
◇	Medium yellow	743	302
◆	Dark yellow	783	306
V	Medium blue	813	160
•	Medium pink	957	52
○	Orange	722	323
	Black*	310	403
	*Eyes are French knots done in black.		

2. Stitch

Follow the cross-stitching instructions given in Cross-Stitch Basics.

If you cannot locate a bib premade with an Aida insert, cross-stitch the design on a strip of Aida or on Ribband and finish according to following instructions.

3. Finish

Note: The bib premade with an insert requires no finishing.

If adding a cross-stitched panel to a plain bib, follow the instructions below. Measurements assume a bib with a 10-inch-wide front; adjust as necessary for smaller or larger sizes.

■ After cross-stitching the design on Aida, cut off 1 inch of the fabric around all four edges. If stitching is done on Ribband, cut 1 inch off only the ends.

■ Fold back the Aida fabric or Ribband ½ inch on each end of the cross-stitched design. Press the folds with an iron to crease; stitch.

■ Center cross-stitched piece on the bib and sew in place.

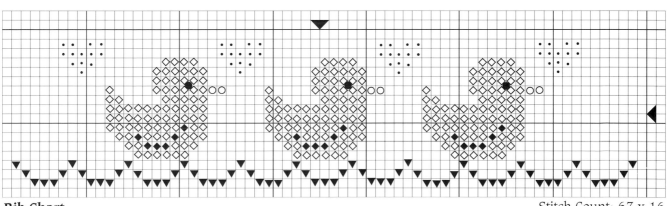

Bib Chart

Stitch Count: 67 x 16

Heart-Shaped Pillow

1. Gather Materials

Heart-shaped, Soft Touch pillow cover:
Premade with 14-count Aida front, EZ
Stitch back, 10x12 inches plus 3-inch
ruffle (Charles Craft, PS5570-6750),
or plain pillow with at least a 7x7½-inch
front and the following materials:
   Aida fabric: 14 count, white, 10x10½
    inches
   Washable fabric glue
Satin ribbon: ⅜x10 inches (optional)
Heart-shaped pillow form
Tapestry needle
Scissors
Needle and sewing thread (optional)

2. Stitch

Reach inside the EZ Stitch pillow back to
cross-stitch the design. Follow the cross-
stitching instructions for stitching over two
squares given in Cross-Stitch Basics. Use
the alphabet on page 169 to personalize
the pillow. Use four strands of floss
throughout.

If you cannot locate a pillow premade
with an Aida front, cross-stitch the design
on Aida fabric and finish according to
following instructions.

3. Finish

Note: The pillow premade with an Aida
front requires no finishing. Just insert
pillow form after cross-stitching design.
You may wish to whipstitch the opening in
the pillow back closed; do not glue it shut
or you will not be able to remove the
pillow form to wash the pillowcase. If
desired, make a simple bow from ribbon;
tack at top of pillow (see photo, page 25).

If adding a cross-stitched panel to a plain
pillow, follow the instructions below.
■ After cross-stitching design on Aida, cut
off 1 inch of fabric from all sides, leaving

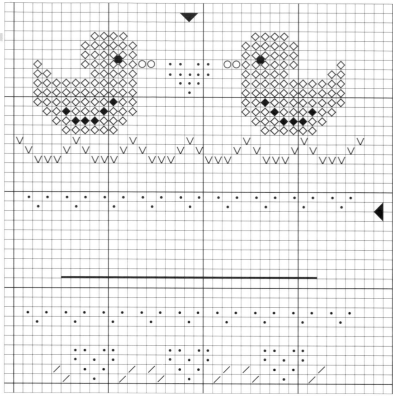

Pillow Chart

Stitch Count: 37 x 37

Floss: (Symbol indicates color on chart.)

Symbol	Color name	DMC #	Anchor #
◇	Medium yellow	743	302
◆	Dark yellow	783	306
○	Orange	722	323
•	Medium pink	957	52
	Dark pink*	956	42
V	Medium blue	813	160
/	Light green	703	238
	Black*	310	403

*Personalize with dark pink.
Eyes are French knots done in black.

an 8x8½-inch piece of cross-stitched fabric.
■ Fold back the Aida fabric ½ inch on all
four sides of the cross-stitched design.
Press the folds with an iron to crease.
■ Trim excess fabric away at the corners,
cutting at a 45-degree angle.
■ Unfold fabric; apply an even coat of glue
to each flap. Smooth flaps firmly into place;
allow to dry. Or, stitch flaps down.
■ Apply fabric glue to entire back of cross-
stitched Aida; center it on front of pillow
and press in place (pin down until glue
dries, if necessary). As an alternative to
gluing cross-stitched piece, you can sew it
to the pillow.
■ Insert pillow form; if desired, whipstitch
opening in back of pillow closed.

Receiving Blanket

1. Gather Materials

Rainbow receiving blanket: 16 count, 32x38 inches (Charles Craft, AF7600-5738), *or* the following materials:

> **Even-weave fabric:** Anne cloth from Leisure Arts *or* other even-weave afghan fabric that will feel soft next to baby, 14 or 16 count, 32x38 inches
>
> **Binding:** White or color to match fabric, 1 inch x 4 yards
>
> **Thread to match binding**
>
> **Sewing machine**

Tapestry needle
Scissors

2. Stitch

Follow the cross-stitching instructions for stitching over two squares given in Cross-Stitch Basics. Use all six strands of floss for stitching.

Note: Don't let the diagonal stitching confuse you. It is still done on the squares of the fabric, but the graph is designed to give the appearance of diagonal stitching. Hold the blanket with the lower left corner in your left hand; begin stitching the design at the bottom of the chart about 1 inch in from the colored band on the bottom and side of the blanket.

3. Finish

Note: The premade receiving blanket requires no finishing.

If you cannot locate a premade receiving blanket of even-weave fabric, you can make one following the instructions below. Cross-stitch the design after the blanket is made.

■ Cut the even-weave fabric to 32x38 inches. If using afghan fabric, extend the measurements to include the full repeats (squares) of the fabric design. If rounded corners are desired, use a jar lid or the top of a drinking glass as a pattern; place it in each corner of the fabric, trace with chalk or pencil, and cut off excess fabric.

■ Stitch the binding around the edge of the fabric, following directions on the package.

Floss: (Symbol indicates color on chart.)

Symbol	Color name	DMC #	Anchor #
◇	Medium yellow	743	302
◆	Dark yellow	783	306
◯	Orange	722	323
•	Medium pink	957	52
V	Medium blue	813	160
■	Black*	310	403

*Backstitch around eye with one strand of black.

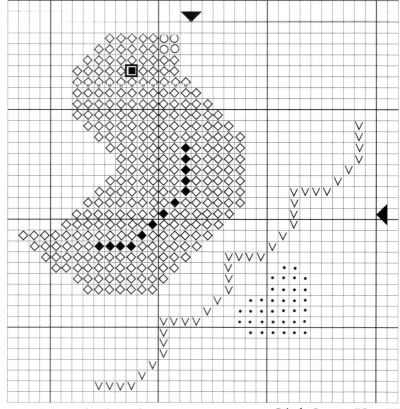

Receiving Blanket Chart   Stitch Count: 32 x 33

Needle Case,
page 32

Rose Pin,
page 31

Rose Pin

1. Gather Materials

Perforated paper: 14 count, gold, 4 inches square (Yarn Tree Designs, Inc.)

Felt or decorative paper: Pink, 2½ inches square

Pin back: 1¼ inches long

Glass seed beads: Light pink, medium pink, dark pink, light green, and dark green (Mill Hill Glass Seed Beads, Gay Bowles Sales)

Thick, white glue

Glue gun or strong glue for metal

Quilting needle: No. 11

Scissors

2. Stitch

Follow the instructions for stitching with beads and for using perforated paper given in Cross-Stitch Basics. Use a single strand of floss in the same color as the bead. If desired, the design can be stitched without beads using three strands of floss and making full cross-stitches.

3. Finish

■ Carefully cut off the excess paper around the design, cutting through the first row of holes just beyond the stitching (the first holes without thread through them).

■ Use the pattern, right, to cut a felt or decorative paper backing for the design. It should be about ¹⁄₁₆ inch smaller than the perforated paper. Spread a thin layer of thick, white glue on the backing, and put it on the back of the stitched perforated paper.

■ Glue the pin back in the center of the back of the pin using a glue gun or other strong glue.

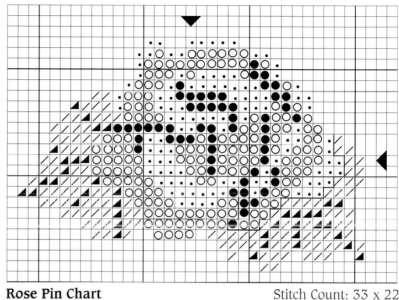

Rose Pin Chart   Stitch Count: 33 x 22

Floss: (Symbol indicates color of floss & bead on chart.)

Symbol	Color name	DMC #	Anchor #	Bead #
•	Light pink	776	74	145
○	Medium pink	3733	76	2005
●	Dark pink	3731	77	553
/	Light green	912	205	525
◢	Dark green	910	229	2020

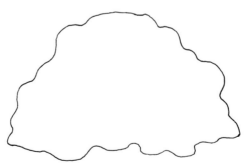

Rose Pin
Full-Size Pattern

Needle Case

1. Gather Materials

Aida fabric: 14 count, white, 7¼ inches
   square
Satin fabric: Pink, ⅛x24 inches
Felt: White, 2½ inches square
**Washable fabric glue or sewing needle
   and white thread**
Scissors
Tapestry needle
Iron

2. Stitch

This design is cross-stitched on the
diagonal, with one corner of the design in
the center of each side of the Aida; before
cross-stitching, fold the fabric to find the
center of each side and crease or pin the
edge at that point. Draw very light pencil
lines to connect these points (diagram A).
Cross-stitching will be done about ¾ inch in
from these pencil lines; be sure to count
your stitch placement carefully, using the
pencil lines to correspond to the edges of
the graph. Follow the cross-stitching
instructions given in Cross-Stitch Basics.

3. Finish

■ After cross-stitching the design, cut off
the excess fabric following the pencil lines
(diagram B).
■ Lay Aida fabric with wrong side up,
design side down. Fold up ½ inch on each
side and press with iron to crease; unfold
(diagram C).

■ Fold each corner in toward center,
folding across the point at which the two
side creases meet (diagram D); press with
iron.
■ Fold in the four sides on the creases
previously ironed in place. This leaves four
mitered corners with no raw edges
(diagram E).
■ Cut ribbon in four 6-inch lengths. Glue
or stitch the end of a piece of ribbon under
the Aida fabric at each corner, extending
the remaining ribbon straight out from
each point (diagram F).
■ Glue or whipstitch down each side;
if stitching, being careful not to stitch
through the Aida to the design side.
■ Lay satin lining wrong side up; fold up
½ inch on each side as you did the Aida
fabric. Press with iron to crease; unfold.
Fold in each corner, folding across the
point at which the two side creases meet
(diagram G); press with iron. Fold in the
four sides on the creases previously ironed
in place. This leaves four mitered corners
as on the Aida fabric.
■ Turn satin right side up and center over
wrong side of Aida fabric (Aida will be
about ⅛ inch larger than satin). Whipstitch
satin to Aida (diagram H).
■ Glue edges only or whipstitch felt piece
to satin with the points of the felt at the
center of each side of the satin (diagram I).
Fold in each corner of the Aida so the
points meet in the center of the felt square;
press with iron to crease.
■ Tie all ribbons together in a simple bow
(diagram J).
■ To use, untie ribbons and run needles in
and out of felt (diagram K).

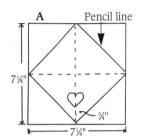

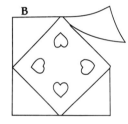

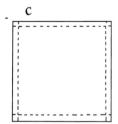

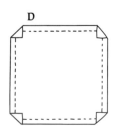

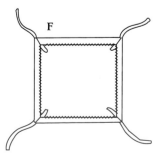

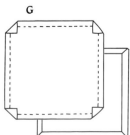

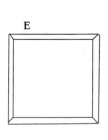

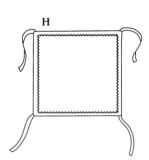

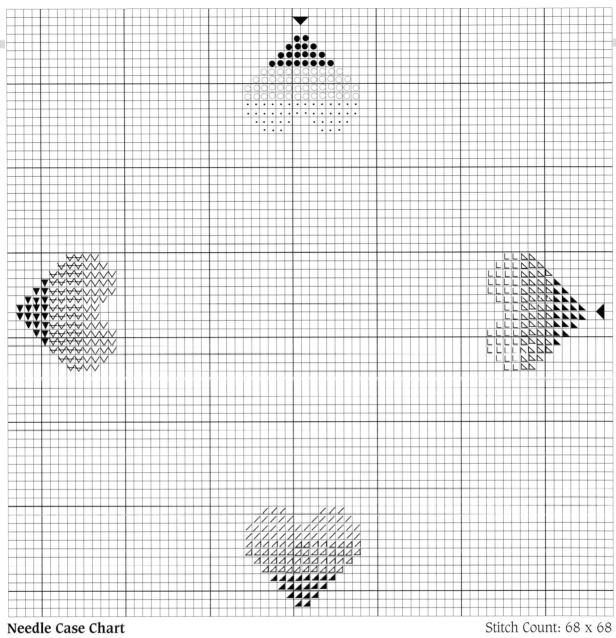

Needle Case Chart

Stitch Count: 68 x 68

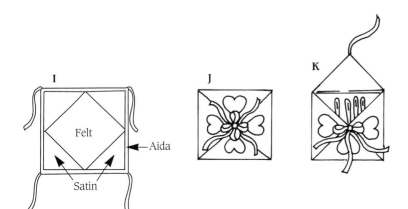

Floss: (Symbol indicated color on chart.)

Symbol	Color name	DMC #	Anchor #
•	Light pink	3716	50
○	Medium pink	957	52
●	Dark pink	956	54
/	Light green	912	243
◿	Medium green	909	245
◢	Dark green	890	246
L	Light lavender	210	108
◺	Medium lavender	209	109
◣	Dark lavender	208	110
V	Light blue	799	145
▽	Medium blue	798	146
▼	Dark blue	797	148

Just Because

Miniwreath,
page 36

Bookmark,
page 35

Always
Friends

Friends
are
Special

GULLIVER'S TRAVELS

10

and held his hand in a posture to show that I must be c...
as a prisoner. However, he made other signs to let me...
stand that I should have meat and drink enough, and...
good treatment. Whereupon I once more thought of att...
ing to break my bonds, but again, when I felt the sma...
their arrows upon my face and hands, which were...
blisters, and many of the darts still sticking in them...
observing likewise that the number of my enemies incr...
I gave tokens to let them know that they might do wi...
what they pleased. Upon this the *Hurgo* and his train...
drew with much civility and cheerful countenances...
after I heard a general shout, with frequent repetitions...
words, *Peplom selan,* and I felt great numbers of the P...
on my left side relaxing the cords to such a degree, th...
was able to turn upon my right, and to ease myself...
making water; which I very plentifully did, to the...
astonishment of the people, who conjecturing by my mo...
what I was going to do, immediately opened to the righ...
left on that side, to avoid the torrent which fell with...
noise and violence from me. But before this, they had da...
my face and both my hands with a sort of ointment...
pleasant to the smell, which in a few minutes removed a...
smart of their arrows. These circumstances, added to...
...I received by their victuals and drink, w...

A VOYAGE

This resolution perhaps...
gerous, and I am confide...
prince in Europe on the l...
it was extremely prude...
these people had endea...
arrows while I was as...
with the first sense o...
my rage and stren...
strings wherewith...
able to make resis...

These people a...
to a great perf...
encouragement...
of learning. ...
wheels for th...
often build...
feet long,...
carried of...
sea. Fiv...
set at w...
frame of w...
seven feet long at...
wheels. The shout I hea...

Bookmark

1. Gather Materials

Aida fabric: 14 count, white, 6x9½ inches
Cluny lace: White, ½x8 inches
Feather-edged ribbon: Pink, ½x10 inches
Thick, white glue
Scissors
Tapestry needle
Iron

2. Stitch

Follow the cross-stitching instructions given in Cross-Stitch Basics.

3. Finish

■ After cross-stitching the design on Aida, cut 1 inch of fabric off all four sides, leaving a 4x7½-inch piece of fabric. Place it design side up on your work surface.

■ Glue a 4-inch length of cluny lace at top and bottom of bookmark, extending it out above and below the fabric and keeping it flush with the sides.

■ Glue a 5-inch length of ribbon centered over the glued edge of the lace and the Aida fabric, with ½ inch extending beyond each side. Fold the excess ½ inch of ribbon to the back of the Aida and glue or stitch in place. Allow glue to dry.

■ Fold back the fabric on either side of the design until the sides meet in the center of the back. Press the folds with an iron to crease. The bookmark should now be 2 inches wide and 8½ inches high, including the lace.

■ Unfold the fabric, and apply an even coat of glue to the back of each flap; smooth flaps firmly back into place and allow to dry. As an alternative to gluing, you can stitch the flaps down.

Bookmark Chart　　　　　　Stitch Count: 29 x 43

Floss: (Symbol indicates color on chart.)

Symbol	Color name	DMC#	Anchor#
▼	Dark Blue*	930	922
·	Light Pink	818	49
○	Medium Pink	224	893
●	Dark Pink	223	895
	*Backstitch lettering with dark blue.		

Miniwreath

1. Gather Materials

Aida fabric: 14 count, white, 8 inches square
Stik 'N Puff: 4-inch round (BANAR DESIGNS, Inc.) *or* circle pattern, below, and the following materials:
  Cardboard: Heavyweight, 4-inch circle
  Batting: 4-inch square
  Thick, white glue
Satin ribbon: Pink, ⅜x60 inches
Rattail cord: Pink, 16 inches
Wreath: Grapevine, 6 inches in diameter with 4-inch opening
Dried florals: Baby's breath or gypsophila
Glue gun or thick, white glue
Scissors
Tapestry needle

2. Stitch

Follow the cross-stitching instructions given in Cross-Stitch Basics.

3. Finish

Finishing instructions for covering padded shapes are given in General Project Instructions. The following are additional instructions for this project.

■ If you do not have a Stik 'N Puff, cut a 4-inch circle from the cardboard and from batting.

■ Cover the Stik 'N Puff with the cross-stitched Aida fabric or cover the cardboard circle with the batting circle, then the cross-stitched Aida fabric.

■ Glue the rattail cord around the edge of the covered circle.

■ Wrap the satin ribbon around the grapevine wreath six to eight times. Tie the ends in a simple bow at the top of the wreath.

■ Turn wreath face down. Glue padded circle to back of wreath with cross-stitched design facing front and top of design at top of wreath (bow). Turn wreath right side up and allow to dry.

■ Separate dried florals into 12 to 18 small pieces (about 1 inch across). Glue onto front of wreath, pushing stem ends into wreath on either side of ribbon (see photo, page 34).

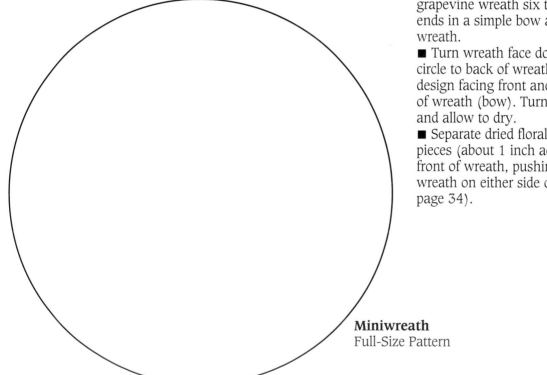

Miniwreath
Full-Size Pattern

Floss: (Symbol indicates color on chart.)

Symbol	Color name	DMC#	Anchor#
•	Light Pink	818	49
○	Medium Pink	223	893
●	Dark Pink	3731	77
	Burgundy*	814	44
×	Light Brown	435	369
✳	Medium Brown	975	370
		Beige	437	368

*Backstitch lettering, ribbon, and bow with burgundy.

Miniwreath Chart

Stitch Count: 30 x 34

For Teacher

Chalkboard Magnet
or Pin, page 39

Bookmark,
page 40

Sampler,
page 39

Chalkboard Magnet or Pin

1. Gather Materials

Perforated paper: 14 count, gold, 2 inches square (Yarn Tree Designs, Inc.)
Felt or decorative paper: Red, 1½ inches square
Miniature chalkboard: 2x3 inches
Acrylic paint: White
Paintbrush: Small, round
Transfer (carbon) paper
Magnet: With adhesive backing, about 1 inch square, *or* pin back: 1¼ inches long
Glass seed beads: Light red, dark red, green, and white (Mill Hill Glass Seed Beads, Gay Bowles Sales)
Thick, white glue
Glue gun or strong glue for metal
Quilting needle: No. 11
Scissors

2. Stitch

Follow the instructions for stitching with beads and for using perforated paper given in Cross-Stitch Basics. Use a single strand of floss in the same color as the bead. If desired, the design can be stitched without beads using three strands of floss and making full cross-stitches.

3. Finish

■ Carefully cut off the excess paper around the design, cutting through the first row of holes just beyond the cross-stitching (the first holes without thread in them).
■ Trace the words "#1 Teacher" on the chalkboard using transfer paper. Use the paint brush to paint the traced words with white acrylic paint; allow to dry.
■ Glue the cross-stitched apple to the lower right corner of the chalkboard frame (see photo, page 38).

■ For a pin, glue the pin back onto the center back of the chalkboard using a glue gun or strong glue for metal. For a magnet, peel the protective paper off the back of the magnet; firmly press the adhesive side onto the center back of the chalkboard.

Chalkboard Magnet or Pin
Full-Size Painting Pattern

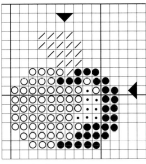

Chalkboard Magnet or Pin Chart

Stitch Count: 12 x 13

Floss: (Symbol indicates color on chart.)

Symbol	Color name	DMC#	Anchor#	Bead
○	Light Red	321	47	2013
●	Dark Red	498	20	367
/	Green	702	258	167
·	White		1	479

Sampler

1. Gather Materials

Aida fabric: 14 count, white, 5 inches square
Frame: With 2-inch-square opening
Backing board: 3 inches square, with peel-and-stick surface, *or* heavyweight cardboard and thick, white glue
Glue gun, thick, white glue, or strapping tape
Scissors
Tapestry needle

2. Stitch

Follow the cross-stitching instructions given in Cross-Stitch Basics.

3. Finish

■ After cross-stitching the design on Aida, cut off 1 inch of the fabric on all four sides,

(continued)

Sampler
(continued)

leaving a 3-inch square of cross-stitched fabric.

■ Press fabric smoothly onto adhesive side of peel-and-stick backing board (if using plain cardboard, apply an even layer of glue to the cardboard; press fabric into it).

■ Center the design in the frame opening. Use glue gun, thick, white glue, or strapping tape to secure the design to the back of the frame.

Sampler Chart   Stitch Count: 28 x 25

Floss: (Symbol indicates color on chart.)

Symbol	Color Name	DMC#	Anchor#
○	Medium Red	321	47
●	Dark Red*	498	20
/	Green*	912	205
·	Pink*	818	49
	Dark Brown*	433	371

*Backstitch the letters with two strands of dark red, the hearts with one strand of pink, the leaves with one strand of green, and the stems with dark brown.

Bookmark

1. Gather Materials

Aida fabric: 14 count, white, 7x9½ inches
Thick, white glue
Scissors
Tapestry needle
Iron

Bookmark Chart   Stitch Count: 25 x 36

Floss: (Symbol indicates color on chart.)

Symbol	Color name	DMC#	Anchor#
○	Medium Red	321	47
●	Dark Red	498	20
▼	Dark Blue*	798	146
×	Beige	437	368
/	Medium Green	912	205
	Black*	310	403
V	Light Blue	799	145
◢	Dark Green	910	229

*Backstitch everything, except lettering, with black. Backstitch lettering with two strands of dark blue.

2. Stitch

Follow the cross-stitching instructions given in Cross-Stitch Basics.

3. Finish

■ After cross-stitching the design on Aida, cut 1 inch of fabric off all four sides, leaving a 5x7½-inch piece of fabric.

■ Fringe the top and bottom ½ inch by pulling out the horizontal threads.

■ Fold back the fabric on either side of the design until the sides meet in the center of the back. Press the folds with an iron to crease. The bookmark should now be 2½ inches wide and 7½ inches high, including the fringe.

■ Unfold fabric, and apply an even coat of glue to the back of each flap; smooth flaps firmly back into place and allow to dry. As an alternative to gluing, stitch flaps down.

Best Friend

Kitty Place Mat,
page 42

PURRRRSONALLY YOURS

KITTY

Dog Collar,
page 43

Kitty Place Mat

1. Gather Materials

Vinyl Aida place mat: White, 12x18
  inches (Crafter's Pride)
Scissors
Tapestry needle

2. Stitch

Start cross-stitching ¾ inch in from both
sides, following the cross-stitching
instructions given in Cross-Stitch Basics.
Use the alphabet on page 170 to stitch
your own kitty's name in the upper right
corner of the mat.

3. Finish

Note: No finishing is necessary with vinyl
Aida. If you would like to have rounded
corners on the mat, place a jar lid or top of
a glass in a corner just touching each side;
trace around it with a pencil. Cut off the
excess vinyl Aida. Repeat for each corner.

Floss: (Symbol indicates color on chart)

Symbol	Color name	DMC#	Anchor#
⌄	Light Blue Gray	932	920
▽	Medium Blue Gray	931	921
▶	Dark Blue Gray	930	922
·	Light Gold	745	302
○	Medium Gold	977	303
●	Dark Gold	976	803
■	Black	310	403

Personalize with three shades of a color of
your choice. Eyes are French knots done
in black.

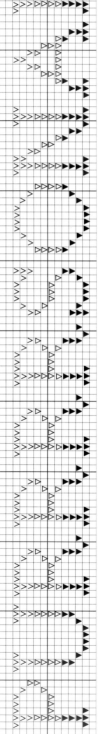

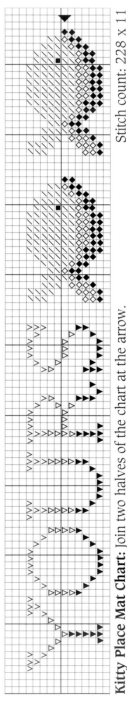

Stitch count: 228 x 11

Kitty Place Mat Chart: Join two halves of the chart at the arrow.

Dog Collar

1. Gather Materials

Ribband: 14 count, ecru, 1x15 inches, with scalloped edge, *or* the following materials:

    Aida fabric: 14 count, white, 4x15 inches

    Ribbon, lace, or rickrack: ⅛x30 inches (optional)

Dog collar: Red, 1x12 inches (or adjust other materials to fit size of smaller or larger collar)

Tapestry needle

Iron

Thick, white glue

Scissors

Sewing machine or needle and thread (optional)

2. Stitch

Follow the cross-stitching instructions given in Cross-Stitch Basics. If you cannot locate Ribband, cross-stitch the design on a strip of Aida fabric and finish according to the following instructions.

3. Finish

Note: This project is intended as an embellishment for a collar used for special occasions, not every day; the cross-stitched fabric will become soiled and worn. (Measurements assume a collar approximately 1x12 inches; adjust as necessary.)

■ After cross-stitching the design on Ribband, cut 1 inch of the fabric off each end. If cross-stitching is done on Aida, cut 1 inch off all four edges.

■ Fold back the Ribband ½ inch on each end of the cross-stitched design; press the folds with an iron to crease. If using Aida fabric, fold back ½ inch on all four sides; cut the corners at a 45-degree angle to allow flaps to lie flat on the back of collar.

■ Hemstitch the folded ends (flaps) or glue them in place. To glue, unfold fabric, and apply an even coat of glue to each flap; smooth flaps firmly into place and allow them to dry.

■ Apply fabric glue to the entire back of the cross-stitched Ribband or Aida; press firmly in place on the collar between the buckle and the holes.

■ If using Aida, glue ribbon, lace, or rickrack along the edges of the fabric (where the Ribband has scalloped edges).

Floss: (Symbol indicates color on chart.)

Symbol	Color name	DMC#	Anchor#
✕	Light Brown	841	388
○	Red	666	46

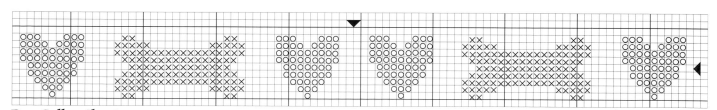

Dog Collar Chart

Stitch Count: 92 x 9

Gifts for Special Occasions

❖ ❖ ❖

Commemorate occasions of sentiment by giving a heartfelt gift crafted with love. Whether it's as simple as a greeting card for a friend's birthday or as elaborate as a photo album for your daughter's wedding, you're sure to find the perfect gift for your special occasion.

Great Day

Gift Bag,
page 46

Tie-On Tag,
page 48

Greeting Card,
page 47

HAPPY BIRTHDAY

Kate

Gift Bag

1. Gather Materials

Perforated paper: White, 4½ inches
  square (Yarn Tree Designs, Inc.)
Satin ribbon: Light blue, ⅛x15 inches
Lace: Flat, white, ½x15 inches
Gift bag: Pink, 8x10 inches
Thick, white glue
Tapestry needle
Scissors

2. Stitch

Follow the instructions given in Cross-Stitch Basics for cross-stitching on perforated paper.

3. Finish

■ Cut ½ inch off all edges of the perforated paper to form a 3½-inch square.
■ Apply an even coat of glue to entire back of cross-stitched perforated paper. Press firmly into center of gift bag.
■ Cut one end of lace at a 45-degree angle. Glue lace around edge of perforated paper, starting at one corner and mitering each corner. When you reach the first corner, cut off the remaining lace at a 45-degree angle.
■ Cut one end of satin ribbon at a 45-degree angle. Glue satin ribbon where perforated paper and lace meet, starting at one corner and mitering each corner. When you reach the starting point, cut off the remaining ribbon at a 45-degree angle.

Gift Bag Chart

Stitch Count: 29 x 40

Floss: (Symbol indicates color on chart.)

Symbol	Color name	DMC #	Anchor #
+	Yellow	3078	292
✳	Gold	743	302
/	Light green	912	205
•	Light pink	818	49
○	Medium pink	957	52
●	Dark pink	3731	77
V	Light blue	932	920
▼	Medium blue	931	921
L	Light lavender	554	108
◣	Medium lavender	553	98
	Dark Green*	910	229

*Backstitch stems with dark green.

Greeting Card

1. Gather Materials

Perforated paper: Gold, 4 inches square (Yarn Tree Designs, Inc.)
Paper doilies: Heart-shaped, 2, white, approximately 3½ inches wide
Plain card or heavy paper to make card: 5x7 inches
Glass seed beads: Pink, light green, medium pink, and dark pink. (Mill Hill Glass Seed Beads, Gay Bowles Sales)
Thick, white glue
Quilting needle: No. 11
Scissors

2. Stitch

Follow the instructions for stitching with beads given in Cross-Stitch Basics. Use a single strand of floss in the same color as the bead. If desired, the design can be stitched without beads using two strands of floss and making full cross-stitches.

3. Finish

■ Use a doily to make a pattern by tracing the heart shape of the doily just inside the "lace" edge.
■ Center the pattern over the beading. Cut away excess perforated paper.
■ Apply an even coat of glue to entire back of stitched perforated paper. Place one doily face down centered over the glued perforated paper and press firmly in place. Allow glue to dry.
■ Glue plain doily near the top left edge of the card. Glue the cross-stitched heart with the doily backing at the lower right of the card, overlapping the plain doily slightly. Allow glue to dry.

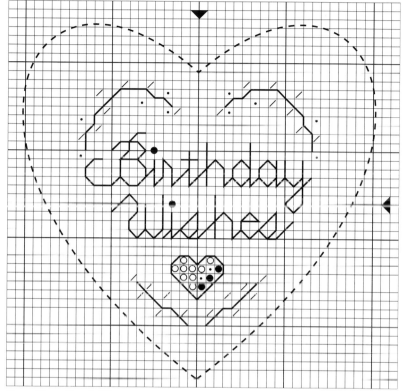

Greeting Card Chart Stitch Count: 28 x 28

Floss and beads: (Symbol indicates color on chart.)

Symbol	Color name	DMC #	Anchor #	Bead #
•	Pink	776	74	2018
/	Light Green	702	258	167
○	Medium Pink	3733	76	2005
●	Dark Pink*	3731	77	553
	Black*	310	403	
	Dark Green*	500	879	

*Backstitch letters with two strands of black. Use one strand of dark green for stems and one strand of dark pink to outline heart.

Tie-On Tag

1. Gather Materials

Perforated paper: White, 4½x2 inches
(Yarn Tree Designs, Inc.)
Gift wrap: Same as used to wrap package,
4½x2 inches
Ribbon or lace: ⅛ inch or ¼ inch wide
(optional)
Thick, white glue
Scissors
Paper punch

2. Stitch

Follow the instructions given in Cross-Stitch Basics for cross-stitching on perforated paper. Choose one of the motifs on the charts below and cross-stitch it on the tag. Personalize the tag using one of the alphabets on pages 168 or 169, stitching letters in the color of your choice.

3. Finish

■ Center the pattern over the cross-stitched area of the perforated paper. Cut off excess paper. Note: For long names or messages, extend the length of the tag, as needed, on the end opposite the hole.
■ Cut gift wrap paper slightly smaller (¹⁄₁₆ inch) than pattern. Glue to back of tag.
■ Cut or punch hole near pointed end of tag.
■ Glue ribbon or lace around the edges of the tag, if desired.
■ Thread ribbon through hole and tie tag to gift.

Floss: (Symbol indicates color on chart.)

Symbol	Color name	DMC #	Anchor #
•	Light Pink	957	52
○	Medium Pink	956	54
●	Red	321	47
V	Blue	799	143
L	Lavender	553	98
/	Green	704	237
+	Yellow	307	290
■	Black	310	403

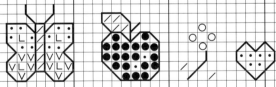

Tie-On Tag Charts

Tie-On Tag Pattern (Extend at right end as needed.)

Made It!

For Graduation

Graduation
Photo Frame,
page 50

Key Chain,
page 52

Graduation Photo Frame

1. Gather Materials

Aida fabric: 14 count, white, 11x13 inches
Photo frame: 8x10 inches with oval cutout *or* heavyweight cardboard, 10x24 inches
Fabric: Coordinating plain or print cotton or cotton/polyester blend to cover the backing and easel, 10x15 inches
Batting: 8x10 inches
Rattail cord: Royal blue, 1½ yards
Thick, white glue and/or glue gun
Scissors
Tapestry needle
Sewing needle and black thread

2. Stitch

Follow the cross-stitching instructions given in Cross-Stitch Basics.

3. Finish

Finishing instructions for covering photo frames are given in General Project Instructions. The following are additional instructions for this frame.
■ If making your own cardboard pieces for the frame, cut two 8x10-inch pieces from the heavyweight cardboard. Trace the oval pattern on this page onto one of the 8x10-inch pieces; cut out the oval. Trace the frame stand pattern onto the remaining cardboard piece; cut out the frame stand.
■ Make a tassel by cutting five 4-inch lengths of black floss (all six strands). Fold the floss in half to form 2-inch lengths. Wrap metallic gold floss around the black floss four or five times about ½ inch from the looped ends; tie the gold floss in a simple knot. Cut off excess ends of the gold floss.
■ Stitch the top of the tassel to the center of the hat with black thread.
■ Cover the photo frame with the cross-stitched Aida fabric.
■ Glue rattail cord around outside edge and inside oval edge before assembling front and back of frame.

Graduation Photo Frame
Full-Size Pattern

Floss: (Symbol indicates color on chart.)

Symbol	Color name	DMC #	Anchor #
V	Light blue	799	145
▼	Dark blue	797	147
×	Brown	839	944
/	Light green	912	205
◢	Dark green*	319	218
—	Light gray	415	398
+	Dark gray	414	235
■	Black*	310	403
	Metallic gold	282	4640

*Backstitch vines with dark green and diploma and hat with black.

Top

Graduation Photo Frame Stand
Full-Size Pattern

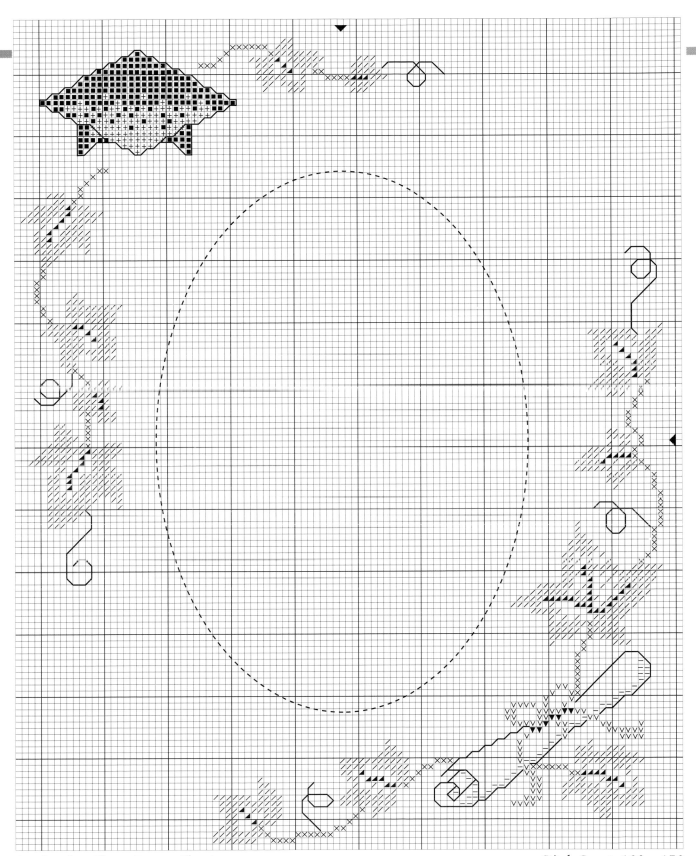

Graduation Photo Frame Chart

Stitch Count: 100 x 130

Key Chain

1. Gather Materials

Aida fabric: 14 count, white, 6 inches
  square
Acrylic key ring/bag tag:
  (Fond Memories, Inc., #BT01)
Thick, white glue
Scissors
Tapestry needle

2. Stitch

Follow the cross-stitching instructions
given in Cross-Stitch Basics.

3. Finish

General assembly instructions are given in
the acrylic key ring package. The following
are additional instructions for this project.
■ After cross-stitching is complete, use the
smaller piece of the acrylic key ring as a
pattern to cut the fabric to size. Center the
acrylic over the design, and trace around it
with a pen. Cut the fabric just inside the
mark.

■ Use the identification card that comes
with the key ring as a backing. Put an
even coat of thick, white glue on the back
of the identification card; press the back of
the stitched fabric firmly onto the glued
tag. Allow glue to dry. Write recipient's
address and telephone number on the
identification tag.
■ Place the fabric, cross-stitched side
down, in the acrylic key ring. Replace the
small piece of acrylic, and press down until
it snaps into place. Assembly is meant to
be permanent.

Floss: (Symbol indicates color on chart.)

Symbol	Color name	DMC #	Anchor #
●	Red*	498	43
V	Blue	799	146
○	Pink	957	52
■	Black*	310	403
	Dark gray*	414	235

*Backstitch the exhaust smoke with one
strand of dark gray, the car with one
strand of black, and the letters with two
strands of red.

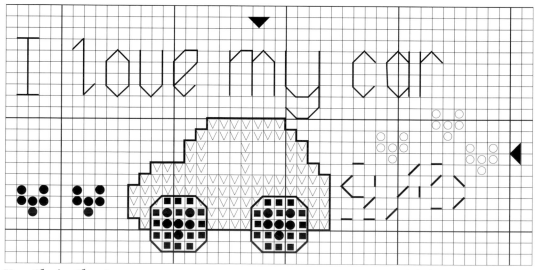

Key Chain Chart   Stitch Count: 43 x 19

Plans and Dreams

Wedding Shower Photo
Frame, page 54

JOIN US

Keepsake Box,
page 54

Keepsake Box

1. Gather Materials

Aida fabric: 14 count, ivory, 8 inches square
Oval bandbox: Approximately 3¼ inches wide and 5 inches long
Cardboard: Heavyweight, 6 inches square (or as large as lid of bandbox)
Batting: 6 inches square
Thick, white glue
Twisted cord: Pink, ¼x30 inches
Scissors
Tapestry needle

2. Stitch

Follow the cross-stitching instructions given in Cross-Stitch Basics.

3. Finish

Finishing instructions for covering padded shapes are given in General Project Instructions. The following are additional instructions for this project.
■ Trace around the top of the box to make an oval pattern the same size as the box. Use the pattern to cut ovals from the cardboard and the batting.
■ Cut the cross-stitched Aida fabric about 1 inch larger than the pattern.
■ Place the batting oval on the cardboard oval and cover both with the cross-stitched Aida fabric.
■ Glue the padded oval on the top of the box.
■ Glue twisted cord around the oval where the padded shape meets the box, starting with the center of the cord at the center top of the design. When ends of cord meet at bottom of design, tie them in a bow. Tie simple knots near the ends of the cord to keep the cord from untwisting.

Wedding Shower Photo Frame

(Photo Frame Chart on page 56)

1. Gather Materials

Perforated paper: 14 count, ivory, 6 inches square (Yarn Tree Designs, Inc.)
Photo frame: 4¼-inch-round opening
Construction paper: Off-white, 6 inches square
Poster board: 6 inches square
Scrap paper: Lightweight, 6 inches square
Thick, white glue and/or glue gun
Scissors
Tapestry needle

2. Stitch

Follow the instructions for cross-stitching on perforated paper given in Cross-Stitch Basics.

3. Finish

■ Since the opening in the back of photo frames varies, use scrap paper to make a pattern to fit your particular frame. Turn the frame face down on a table. Lay the scrap paper over the back of the frame and press it into the indentation to make a crease in the circular shape of the back. Cut out the pattern on the crease.
■ Center the circle pattern over the perforated paper, making sure the stitching is in the center of the circle. Cut off excess perforated paper.
■ Carefully cut out the center of the perforated paper where the picture will be seen. Start by putting the point of the scissors—small, sharp-pointed scissors are best—through the center of the perforated paper and cutting about a 1-inch circle out of the center. Cut from the center hole toward the stitching in several places, like spokes on a wheel, being careful not to cut too close to the cross-stitching. These small

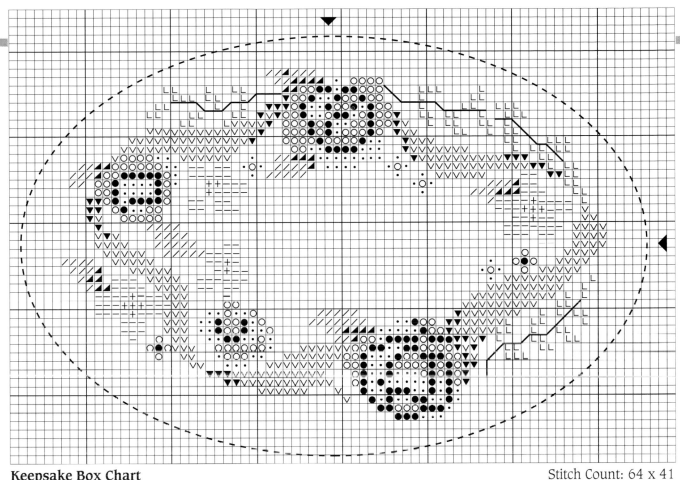

Keepsake Box Chart

Stitch Count: 64 x 41

slits will allow you to manipulate your scissors better when cutting near the cross-stitching. Starting at a slit, cut the perforated paper toward the stitching, stopping at the first hole outside the design that does not have thread through it. Cut around the design, staying in that first row of holes without thread in them, paying special attention when turning corners.

■ After the center paper is completely cut out, trace the perforated paper opening onto the construction paper. Cut out just inside the pencil marks so the construction paper is slightly smaller than the perforated paper.

■ Spread an even layer of white glue on the construction paper. Put stitched perforated paper over the construction paper, matching the cutting lines in the center, so that the construction paper does not show beneath the edges of the perforated paper. Allow glue to dry.

■ Place the picture you are framing

(continued)

Floss: (Symbol indicates color on chart.)

Symbol	Color name	DMC #	Anchor #
•	Light pink	224	893
○	Medium pink	223	895
●	Dark pink	3731	77
V	Light blue	932	920
▼	Dark blue	930	922
L	Light lavender	554	108
∣	Light yellow	3078	292
+	Dark yellow	743	302
╱	Light green	504	875
◢	Dark green	502	877
	Brown*	433	371

*Backstitch the vines with two strands of brown.

Photo Frame
(continued)

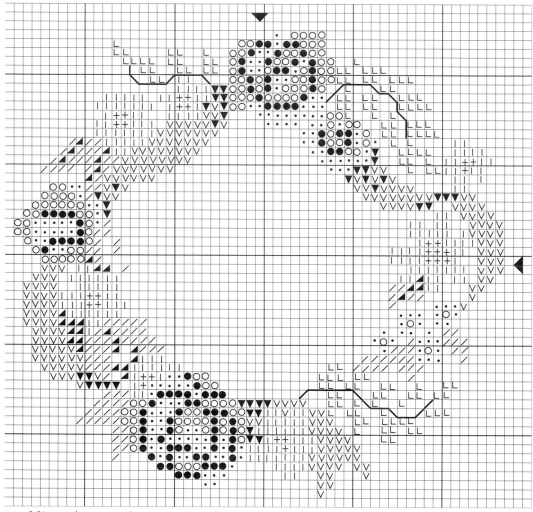

Wedding Shower Photo Frame Chart

Stitch Count: 55 x 52

beneath the papers; make sure the cross-stitched side is up. When you have the photo centered in the opening, trace around the outside of the circle and cut the excess photo off. Glue the photo in place, making sure it shows through the front of the stitched design properly.

■ Place the perforated paper inside the frame with the cross-stitched design facing the front. Cut a poster board piece using the paper pattern to fit the opening in the frame; place in back of the perforated paper and photo, and glue to the frame.

Floss: (Symbol indicates color on chart.)

Symbol	Color name	DMC #	Anchor #
•	Light pink	224	893
○	Medium pink	223	895
●	Dark pink	3731	77
V	Light blue	932	920
▼	Dark blue	930	922
L	Light lavender	554	108
I	Light yellow	3078	292
+	Dark yellow	743	302
/	Light green	504	875
◢	Dark green	502	877
	Brown*	433	371

*Backstitch vines with two strands of brown.

On This Day

Ring Bearer Pillow,
page 58

Pillowcases,
page 58

Wedding Photo Album,
page 60

With this ring
I thee wed
With this ring
I thee wed

On This Day

John and Anne
Davis

June 5, 1992

Ring Bearer Pillow

1. Gather Materials

Ring bearer pillow: Premade with 16-count even-weave front, 7 inches plus 2 inches of gathered lace (Adam Originals), *or* the following materials:

Even-weave fabric: 16 count, ivory, 10 inches square (afghan square with a 4-inch-square or larger stitching area may be used)

Fabric for backing: Ivory moire, 8 inches square

Gathered lace: Ivory, 2x32 inches

Straight pins

Sewing machine, needle, and white thread

Pillow form: 7 inches square (or batting to use as stuffing)

Satin ribbon: Mauve, ⅛x10 inches

Tapestry needle

Scissors

2. Stitch

Unzip the premade pillow and reach inside to stitch the design. Follow the cross-stitching instructions given in Cross-Stitch Basics.

If you cannot locate a pillow premade with an even-weave front, cut a 10-inch-square pillow front from the even-weave fabric. If you are using an afghan square, be sure to center the afghan design within the 10-inch square needed for the pillow. Cross-stitch the design on the even-weave fabric and finish according to following instructions.

3. Finish

Note: The pillow premade with even-weave front requires no finishing. Just insert pillow form after cross-stitching the design, and zip shut.

If making a pillow, use the following instructions.

- Cut an 8-inch square of moire for the back of the pillow.
- Place the cross-stitched front, design side up, on your work surface.
- Place the lace on top of the cross-stitched fabric with the gathered edge of the lace at the raw edge of the fabric; pin in place as you go. Pinch together extra lace at the corners to avoid puckering when the pillow is turned. When you return to the starting point, leave a ½-inch overlap of lace and cut off the excess.
- Place the backing piece on top of the lace with right side down; pin.
- When all layers are assembled, stitch pillow together with ½-inch seams, leaving one side open for turning. Remove pins, and turn the pillow right side out.
- Stitch the center of the ribbon in the center of the pillow. Tie the ribbon in a simple bow; it will hold the rings during the ceremony.
- Insert pillow form. Whipstitch the open side closed, making sure to fold in about ½ inch of fabric from the front and back of the pillow and to catch the edge of the lace between them.

Pillowcases

1. Gather Materials

Pillowcases: White with plain or lace edge, 2

Ribband: Two pieces (2x39 inches each), with scalloped edge, *or* the following materials

Aida fabric: 14-count, white, two pieces (4x41 inches each)

Washable lace: For edging, four pieces (¾x36 inches each)

Feather-edged ribbon: Mauve, ¼x72 inches

Sewing machine and white thread

Scissors

Iron

Tapestry needle

Ring Bearer Pillow Chart

Stitch Count: 58 x 58

2. Stitch

Follow the cross-stitching instructions given in the Cross-Stitch Basics. Cross-stitch the design on the Aida strips before sewing it onto the pillowcases.

3. Finish

■ After cross-stitching the Ribband or plain Aida strips, use the following instructions to add a cross-stitched panel to the pillowcases. Measurements assume pillowcases are 18 inches wide across the open end; adjust as necessary for smaller or larger pillowcases. (Note: Repeat design

Floss: (Symbol indicates color on chart.)

Symbol	Color name	DMC #	Anchor #
╱	Green	504	875
•	Pink	223	895
	Dark blue*	930	922
	Dark green*	502	877
	*Backstitch letters with dark blue and vines with dark green.		

at dotted line until entire strip has been stitched.)

■ If cross-stitching is done on Ribband, cut 1 inch off only the ends. If you use plain Aida strips, cut off 1 inch of the fabric around all four sides.

(continued)

Pillowcases
(continued)

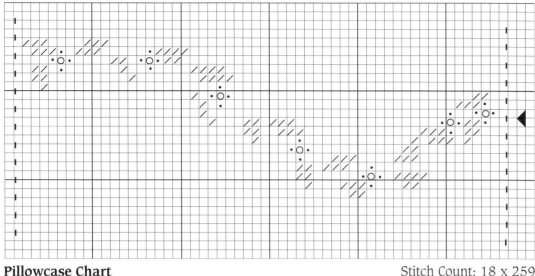

Pillowcase Chart   Stitch Count: 18 x 259
(Repeat design at dotted line until entire strip has been stitched.)

■ Fold back the ends (2-inch width) of Ribband or Aida strips ½ inch; press the folds with an iron to crease.
■ Stitch the fabric flaps down.
■ Starting at the seam of each pillowcase and using the stitched edge of the hem as a placement guide, stitch the Ribband or Aida fabric to the pillowcases.
■ If you use plain Aida fabric, stitch the lace at the top and bottom of the fabric, overlapping the edge of the fabric about ¼ inch.
■ Stitch on the feather-edged ribbon where the lace meets the Aida fabric.

Wedding Photo Album

1. Gather Materials

Aida fabric: 14 count, blue, 8½x10½ inches (Charles Craft)
Photo album: Ring-binder type, approximately 11x12 inches

Floss: (Symbol indicates color on chart.)

Symbol	Color name	DMC #	Anchor #
•	Light pink	224	893
○	Dark pink	3731	77
╱	Medium green	504	875

Cardboard: Heavyweight, 12 inches square
Poster board: Lightweight, 12x24 inches
Batting: 1 inch thick, ⅓ yard, 45 inches wide
Fabric: Satin moire, mauve, ¾ yard (45 inches wide)
Gathered lace: White, 2½ x84 inches, 1½x28 inches
Pearl strings: White, 3 yards
Satin ribbon: Light blue, mauve, and white, ⅜x30 inches each
Glass seed beads: Pink and opalescent white (Mill Hill Glass Seed Beads, Gay Bowles Sales)
Thick, white glue and/or glue gun
Scissors
Tapestry needle

2. Stitch

Follow the instructions for stitching with beads given in Cross-Stitch Basics. Opalescent white beads are used on the doves, and pink beads are stitched on the hearts. Use a single strand of floss in the same color as the bead. If desired, the design can be stitched without beads using two strands of floss in the appropriate color and making full cross-stitches. Personalize the album using the alphabet chart on page 168.

3. Finish

Finishing instructions for covering photo albums and padded shapes are given in General Project Instructions. The following are additional instructions for this album.

■ Cover the album with the moire fabric. Before you glue in the inner linings, cut the three colors of satin ribbon into 15-inch lengths; glue an end of each color ribbon inside the center edge of the album covers to act as ties. Cover the glued ends with the fabric lining.

■ Glue wide lace on the inside of the covers and spine, extending it out 2¼ inches all around.

■ Glue white pearl strings around the covers and spine where the lace meets the moire fabric.

■ Cut 5x7-inch rectangles from batting and cardboard.

■ Cover cardboard rectangle with batting, then cross-stitched Aida fabric.

■ Glue narrow lace on the back of the rectangle, extending it out 1¼ inches.

■ Glue rectangle in center of album front.

■ Glue white pearl strings around the cross-stitched Aida where the lace meets the fabric.

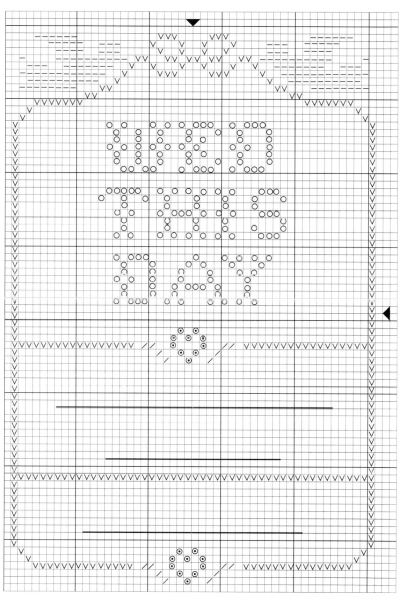

Wedding Photo Album Chart Stitch Count: 50 x 74

Floss: (Symbol indicates color on chart.)

Symbol	Color name	DMC #	Anchor #	Bead #
○	Pink	224	893	
V	Light blue	932	920	
	Dark blue*	3750	922	
/	Green	966	240	
—	Opalescent white beads Snow white	1		2010
⊙	Pink beads	3731	77	553
	*Backstitch lettering with dark blue.			

For the new home

No Place Like Home

Pot Holder,
page 65

Refrigerator
Magnet,
page 63

Welcome Towel,
page 64

Refrigerator Magnet

1. Gather Materials

Aida fabric: 14 count, white, 6 inches square

Lucite House Magnet: (Wheatland Crafts) *or* the following materials:

    Cardboard: Lightweight, 4 inches square

    Felt: Black, 4 inches square

    Magnet: Adhesive backed, 1 inch square

Thick, white glue

Fray Chek (optional)

Scissors

Tapestry needle

2. Stitch

Follow the cross-stitching instructions given in Cross-Stitch Basics.

3. Finish

General assembly instructions are given in the acrylic magnet package. The following are additional instructions for this project, as well as instructions for making the project if you do not have the acrylic magnet.

■ After cross-stitching is complete, use the paper pattern that comes with the magnet to cut the Aida fabric to size. Center the pattern over the stitched design, and trace around it with a pencil. Cut the fabric just inside the mark. Run glue or Fray Chek around the edges after cutting to keep the fabric from fraying; let dry.

■ Use the adhesive-backed cardboard that comes with the magnet as a backing, or cut a cardboard shape using the cross-stitched fabric as a pattern (cut the cardboard about 1/16 inch smaller than the stitched fabric). Put an even coat of thick, white glue on the backing; press the back

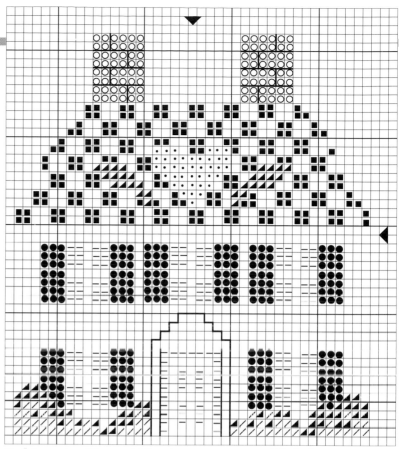

Refrigerator Magnet Chart   Stitch Count: 41 x 46

Floss: (Symbol indicates color on chart.)

Symbol	Color name	DMC #	Anchor #
•	Pink	956	41
○	Red	498	20
╱	Light green	966	214
◢	Dark green	368	214
—	Light gray	415	398
■	Black*	310	403
●	Dark blue	930	922

*Backstitch around door and bricks with one strand of black.

of the stitched fabric firmly onto the glued backing. Allow glue to dry.

■ If you are using the acrylic magnet, place the cross-stitched, cardboard-backed design between the layers of acrylic. Attach the magnet that comes with the acrylic shape. If you are not using the acrylic magnet, cut a backing of felt, and glue or stitch it onto the back of the cardboard. Glue the magnet to the back of the felt.

Welcome Towel

1. Gather Materials

Towel: Premade, white velour, 11x18 inches (fingertip), with 2½x10-inch piece of Aida fabric woven in horizontally (Charles Craft, #VT6900-6750), *or* plain towel without even-weave band and the following materials:

Aida fabric: 14 count, white, 5½x13 inches, *or* Ribband; 2½x13 inches
Washable lace: White, ½x20 inches (if not using Ribband)
Sewing machine or needle and thread
Scissors
Tapestry needle
Iron

2. Stitch

Cross-stitch the design on the Aida band. Follow the cross-stitching instructions given in Cross-Stitch Basics.

If you cannot locate a towel premade with an Aida insert, cross-stitch the design on a strip of Aida fabric or on Ribband and finish according to the following instructions.

3. Finish

Note: The towel premade with the Aida insert requires no finishing. If adding a cross-stitched band to a plain towel using Aida and lace or Ribband, follow the instructions below.

■ After cross-stitching the design on Aida, cut off 1 inch of the fabric from all four sides, leaving a 3½x11-inch piece of stitched fabric. If using Ribband, cut 1 inch off only the ends.
■ Fold back the Aida fabric ½ inch on all four sides of the cross-stitched design. Press the folds with an iron to crease. If using Ribband, fold back only the ends and press.
■ Trim excess Aida fabric away at the corners, cutting at a 45-degree angle.
■ Stitch the flaps in place near the fold with a machine or hemstitch by hand.

Floss: (Symbol indicates color on chart.)

Symbol	Color name	DMC #	Anchor #
V	Blue	932	920
/	Medium green	912	205
	Dark green*	910	229
	Dark pink*	3731	77

*Backstitch vine with dark green and letters with dark pink.

Welcome Towel Chart

Stitch Count: 58 x 29

Pot Holder Chart　　　　　　　　　Stitch count: 55 x 55

■ Center cross-stitched fabric on towel about 3 inches from bottom and sew on with a sewing machine or needle and thread.

■ The Ribband edges are finished; if you use Aida, sew the washable lace on each of the 10-inch edges with about ⅛ inch on the fabric and the rest extending onto the towel.

Pot Holder

1. Gather Materials

Pot holder: Premade, white, quilted, 8 inches square, with 5½x7-inch piece of Aida fabric sewn in (Charles Craft, #PH6200), or plain pot holder without Aida front and the following materials:

Aida fabric: 14 count, white, 8 inches square

Washable ribbon or lace: Dark green or white, 24 inches (optional for trim)

Needle and white thread

Scissors

Tapestry needle

Iron

Sewing machine (optional)

2. Stitch

Cross-stitch the design on the pot holder premade with an Aida insert. Follow the cross-stitching instructions given in Cross-Stitch Basics.

If you cannot locate a pot holder premade with an Aida insert, cross-stitch the design on the Aida fabric square and finish according to the following instructions.

3. Finish

Note: The pot holder premade with the Aida insert requires no finishing. If adding a cross-stitched Aida front to a plain pot holder, follow the instructions below.

■ After cross-stitching the design on Aida,

Floss: (Symbol indicates color on chart.)

Symbol	Color name	DMC #	Anchor #
V	Blue	932	920
/	Medium green	912	205
	Dark green*	910	229
	Dark pink*	3731	77

*Backstitch the vine in dark green and the letters in dark pink.

cut off 1 inch of the fabric from all four sides, leaving a 6-inch square piece of cross-stitched fabric.

■ Fold back the Aida fabric ½ inch on all four sides of the cross-stitched design. Press the folds with an iron to crease.

■ Trim excess Aida fabric away at the corners, cutting at a 45-degree angle.

■ Stitch the flaps in place near the fold with a machine or hemstitch by hand.

■ Center the cross-stitched fabric on the front of the pot holder and stitch in place.

■ To give a more finished appearance, you may want to add a border of ribbon or lace around the Aida fabric. Sew the washable ribbon or lace along each edge of the Aida square with about ⅛ inch on the fabric and the rest extending onto the pot holder.

Little Love

For a Baby Shower

Blanket,
page 69

Bib,
page 67

Tiny T-Shirt,
page 67

Tiny T-Shirt

1. Gather Materials

Waste canvas: 14 count, 3x3½ inch
Infant T-shirt
Rescue tape: 12 inches *or* needle and
   thread
Scissors
Tweezers
Sponge or spray bottle and water
Embroidery needle

2. Stitch

Attach the waste canvas to the front of the
T-shirt following the instructions given in
Cross-Stitch Basics for stitching using
waste canvas. Cross-stitch the heart design
with the top about ½ inch below the
neckline of the shirt. Select an initial from
the alphabet chart on page 171 and stitch
it in the center of the heart.

3. Finish

■ When all cross-stitching is complete,
remove the basting or, if you used Rescue
tape, pull up the edges of waste canvas.
■ Trim the excess waste canvas close to
the cross-stitched design, taking care not to
clip the T-shirt or the stitches.
■ Dampen the waste canvas remaining on
the T-shirt, using a sponge or spray bottle
with plain water, to make the fibers pliable.
■ Use tweezers to pull the horizontal and
vertical waste canvas threads, one at a
time, from beneath the cross-stitching.

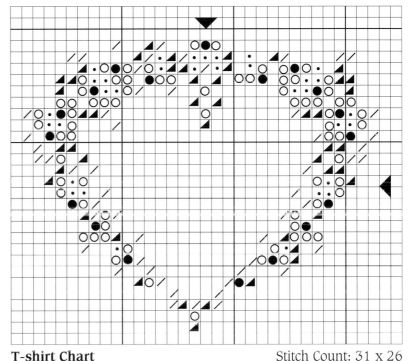

T-shirt Chart   Stitch Count: 31 x 26

Floss: (Symbol indicates color on chart.)

Symbol	Color name	DMC #	Anchor #
•	Light pink	776	73
○	Medium pink	899	40
●	Dark pink	335	41
/	Light green	504	875
◢	Dark green	502	877
	Light blue (for initial)	3325	130

Bib

1. Gather Materials

Bib: White, premade of 14-count Aida
fabric, 5x7 inches (Charles Craft), *or* the
bib pattern on page 68 and the following
materials:

Aida fabric: 14 count, white, 5x7
   inches
Seam binding: White, 48 inches
**Sewing machine or needle and
   thread**
Tapestry needle
Gathered eyelet lace: White, ½x22 inches
   (optional, to sew around edges of bib)
Scissors

(continued)

Bib
(continued)

2. Stitch

Follow the cross-stitching instructions given in Cross-Stitch Basics. Cross-stitch the design 1 inch from bottom edge of bib.

3. Finish

Note: The bib premade with an Aida insert requires no finishing. If you cannot locate a premade Aida bib, you can make one following the instructions below. It is easiest to first make the bib, then cross-stitch it.

■ Using the bib pattern, cut the bib shape from the Aida fabric. Be sure the pattern is placed squarely on the fabric or the cross-stitching will be on an angle.

■ Sew seam binding on the top edge of the bib.

■ Sew remaining binding around outside edge of bib, leaving 13 inches extending from the top on each side to serve as ties.

■ Cross-stitch the design.

■ Sew on the eyelet lace, if desired.

Floss: (Symbol indicates color on chart.)

Symbol	Color name	DMC #	Anchor #
/	Light green	955	203
◢	Dark green*	912	205
•	Light pink	957	52
○	Dark pink*	956	42

*Backstitch heart with dark pink and leaves with dark green.

Bib
Full-Size Pattern

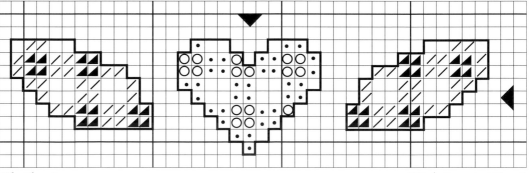

Bib Chart

Stitch Count: 37 x 9

Blanket

1. Gather Materials

Thermal blanket: Pink, 6 count, 32x38 inches (Designing Women, Unlimited), *or* the following materials:

    Thermal fabric: 6 count, 32x38 inches (if you cannot find a thermal fabric, use any blanket and 8.5-count waste canvas)

    Binding: White or color to match fabric, 1 inch x 4 yards

    Thread

    Sewing machine

Tapestry needle

Scissors

2. Stitch

Follow the cross-stitching instructions given in Cross-Stitch Basics, treating the indentations in the thermal weave as the holes in the fabric. Cross-stitch the design centered on one or more sides of the blanket. Use six strands of floss for all stitching.

3. Finish

Note: The premade blanket requires no finishing. If you cannot locate a premade blanket of thermal fabric, you can make one following the instructions below. Cross-stitch the design using 8.5-count waste canvas after the blanket is made; see instructions for stitching with waste canvas given in Cross-Stitch Basics.

■ If necessary, cut the thermal fabric to 32x38 inches. If rounded corners are desired, use a jar lid or top of a drinking glass as a pattern; place it in each corner of the fabric, trace with a chalk or pencil, and cut off excess fabric.

■ Stitch binding around the edge of the blanket, following directions on the package of binding.

Floss: (Symbol indicates color on chart.)

Symbol	Color name	DMC #	Anchor #
/	Light green	955	203
◢	Dark green*	912	205
•	Light pink	957	52
○	Dark pink*	956	742
I	White	Snow white	1

*Backstitch the outlines of the leaves with four strands of dark green and the heart with four strands of dark pink.

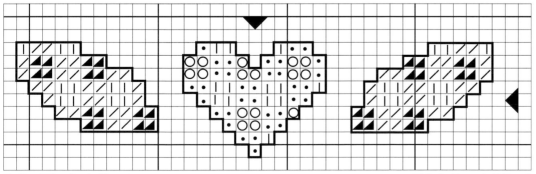

Baby Blanket Chart

Stitch Count: 37 x 9

Captured Moments

Anniversary Photo
Album, page 73

Moments
filled
with
Memories

25

Anniversary Photo Frame,
page 71

Anniversary Photo Frame

1. Gather Materials

Aida fabric: 14 count, white, 8 inches square

Photo frame: 5¼ inches square with heart cutout *or* heavyweight cardboard, 5¼x12 inches (see patterns, right and page 72)

Fabric: White or coordinating plain or print cotton or cotton/polyester blend to cover the frame backing and easel

Batting: 5¼ inches square

Gathered lace: White, 1x24 inches

Rattail cord: Light blue, 12 inches

Glass seed beads: Light pink, medium pink, light blue, dark blue, opalescent white, and gold (Mill Hill Glass Seed Beads, Gay Bowles Sales)

Thick, white glue and/or glue gun

Scissors

Quilting needle: No. 11

2. Stitch

Follow the instructions for stitching with beads given in Cross-Stitch Basics. Choose the appropriate anniversary number and substitute your numbers for those shown on the chart on page 72. Start at the outer edge of the stitch area and work toward the left. Use a single strand of floss in the same color as the bead.

3. Finish

Finishing instructions for covering photo frames are given in General Project Instructions. The following are additional instructions for this frame.
■ Cover the photo frame with the beaded Aida fabric.
■ Glue lace around outside edges and rattail cord around heart opening before assembling front and back of frame.

(continued)

Anniversary Photo Frame
Full-Size Pattern

(Photo Frame Chart on page 72)

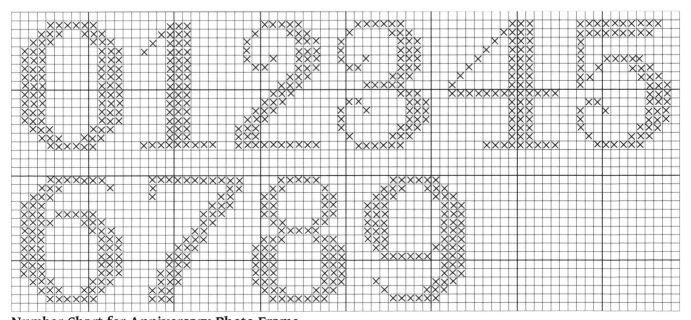

Number Chart for Anniversary Photo Frame

Photo Frame
(continued)

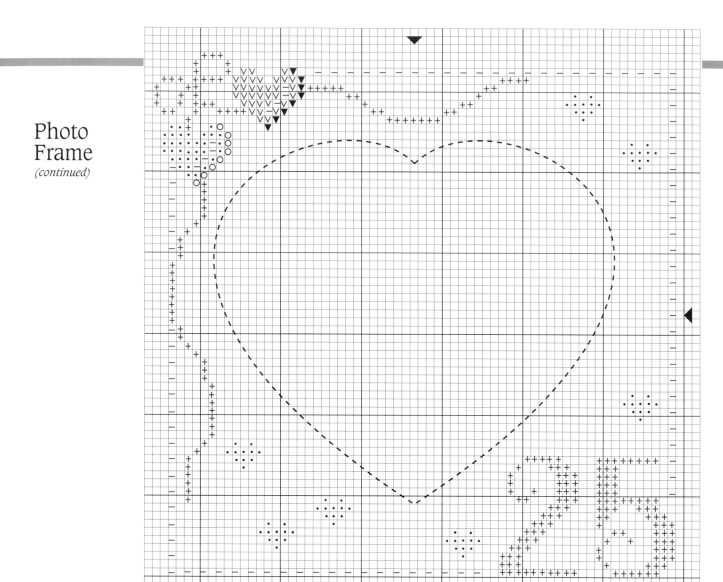

Anniversary Photo Frame Chart

Stitch Count: 65 x 65

Floss: (Symbol indicates color on chart.)

Symbol	Color name	DMC #	Anchor #	Bead #
•	Light pink	818	49	2004
○	Medium pink	957	52	268
V	Light blue	794	120	146
▼	Dark blue	793	121	2006
—	White	Snow white	1	2010
+	Gold	743	302	2011

Top

Anniversary Photo Frame Stand
Full-Size Pattern

Anniversary Photo Album

1. Gather Materials

Aida fabric: 14 count, white, 7½x9 inches
Photo album: Ring-binder type, approximately 11x12 inches
Poster board: Lightweight, 12x24 inches
Cardboard: Heavyweight, 12 inches square
Batting: 1 inch thick, ⅓ yard, 45 inches wide
Fabric: Pink cotton moire, ¾ yard, 45 inches wide
Gathered lace: White, 2 inches x 3½ yards, 1x24 inches
Wire-edged ribbon: White with gold edge, 1x30 inches
Rattail cord: Gold, 24 inches
Small heart appliques
Thick, white glue and/or glue gun
Sewing needle and thread
Scissors
Tapestry needle

2. Stitch

Follow the cross-stitching instructions given in Cross-Stitch Basics.

3. Finish

Finishing instructions for covering photo albums and padded shapes are given in General Project Instructions. The following are additional instructions for this album.
■ Cover the album with the moire fabric.
■ Glue wide lace on inside of covers and spine, extending it out about 1¾ inches.
■ Cut an oval shape (see pattern above) from batting and cardboard.
■ Cover cardboard oval with batting, then with cross-stitched fabric.
■ Glue narrow lace to the back of the oval, extending it out about ¾ inches.
■ Glue covered oval in center of album front.

■ Glue rattail cord around the outside of the oval where the fabric meets the lace.
■ Tie the wire-edged ribbon in a simple bow; glue it above the oval, at the center top of the album. Twist the tails of the ribbon as shown in the photo on page 70, and tack the ends down, taking a small stitch underneath the ribbon. Glue small heart appliques over these stitches.

(Photo Album Chart on page 74)

Floss: (Symbol indicates color on chart.)

Symbol	Color name	DMC #	Anchor #
ᵥ	Pink	818	49
○	Medium pink	957	52
V	Light blue	794	120
▼	Medium blue	793	121
+	Gold*	743	302
+	Metallic gold*	282	4640
	Dark blue*	791	123

*Backstitch lettering with dark blue. Use two strands of gold floss plus one strand of metallic gold for bow and ribbon.

Anniversary Photo Album
Full-Size Pattern

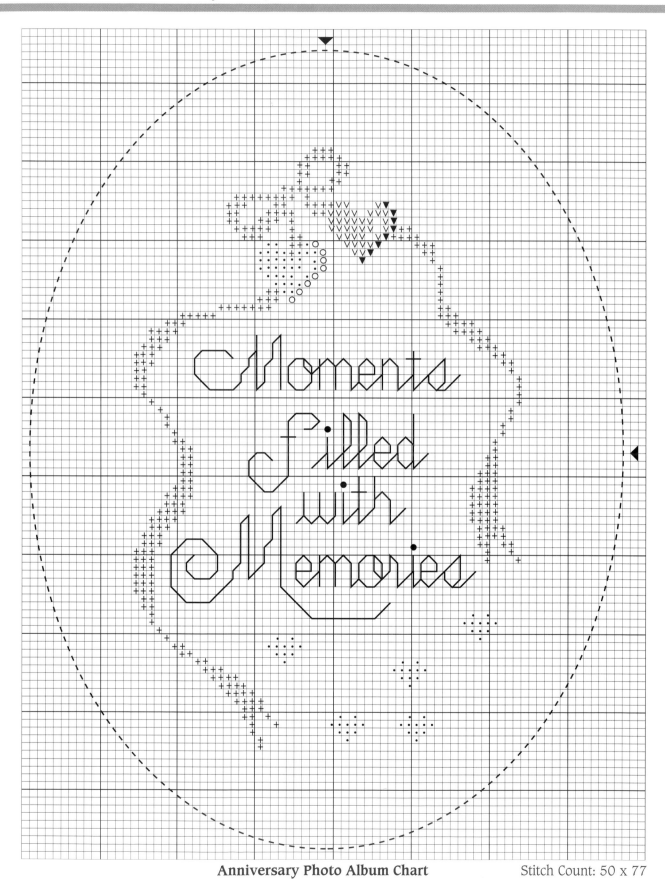

Anniversary Photo Album Chart

Stitch Count: 50 x 77

Gifts for Holidays

❖ ❖ ❖

Trim the year's holidays with fanciful

accessories to decorate the home or to

wear. A Valentine's Day bandbox,

a fun pumpkin pin for Halloween, and

sprightly Santa cones are just a few of

the imaginative gifts to choose from.

Right to the Heart

Bandbox,
page 78

Plant Poke,
page 77

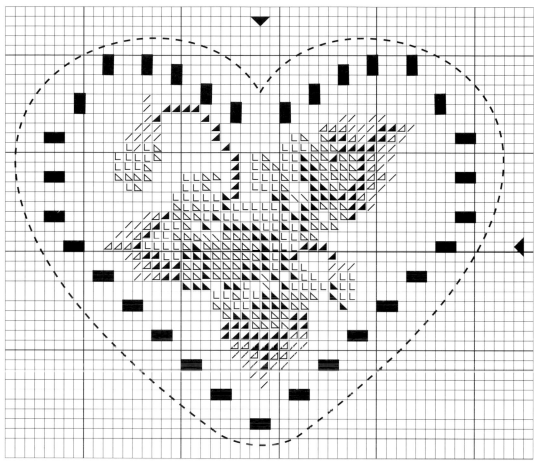

Plant Poke Chart

Stitch Count: 32 x 30

Plant Poke

1. Gather Materials

Perforated paper: Ivory, 5 inches square
(Yarn Tree Designs, Inc.)
Satin ribbon: Lavender, ⅛x18 inches
Cluny lace: Gathered, ecru, ¼x24 inches
Heavyweight cardboard: 4 inches
square, white
Plant stake or wooden dowel: ⅛x12
inches
Thick, white glue
Tapestry needle
Scissors

Floss: (Symbol indicates color on chart.)

Symbol	Color name	DMC #	Anchor #
❘	Light lavender	211	342
◻	Medium lavender	553	109
◤	Dark lavender	552	111
╱	Light green	912	205
◁	Medium green	910	229
◢	Dark green	319	218
╲	Yellow	743	302

2. Stitch

Trace the Plant Poke pattern on page 78
onto the back of the perforated paper,
making sure the rows of holes are straight
up and down and side to side. Cut the
paper about ½ inch larger than the tracing
line (when you are finished cross-stitching,
this excess will be cut off). Follow the
instructions given in Cross-Stitch Basics for
cross-stitching on perforated paper.

(continued)

Plant Poke

(continued)

3. Finish

■ Cut the excess paper off at the pencil line you drew around the heart pattern.

■ With small, sharp-pointed scissors, cut slits in the perforated paper to thread the ⅛-inch ribbon through. The slits should start about ⅛ inch in from the edge of the heart and extend toward the center of the heart, connecting two holes on the diagonal or three holes in a row (see chart, page 77). The slits will be approximately ⅜ inch apart, roughly every three holes.

Plant Poke
Full-Size Pattern

■ Thread the ⅛-inch ribbon through the slits. Start at the bottom point of the heart, and pull about half the ribbon through that slit. Weave each end of the ribbon in and out of the slits until you reach the top of the heart. (If you have trouble getting the ribbon through the slits, fold a piece of tape around the end of the ribbon and cut it on an angle to form a smooth, sharp point.) Both ends of the ribbon should be on the front (cross-stitched) side of the heart; if not, cut extra slits and bring the ribbon ends to the front. Tie a simple bow, and cut off the excess ribbon.

■ Use the pattern to cut a heart from the white cardboard.

■ Glue the lace to the cardboard heart with most of the lace extending out beyond the cardboard; start and end at the V at the top of the heart.

■ Spread an even layer of glue on the side of the cardboard with the lace glued to it. Place the dowel or plant stake end between the perforated paper and cardboard hearts; press hearts together.

Bandbox

1. Gather Materials

Aida fabric: 14 count, white, 6 inches square

Stik 'N Puff: 2-inch heart (BANAR DESIGNS, Inc.) *or* Cardboard and Batting Pattern on page 79 and the following materials:

> **Cardboard:** Heavyweight, 3 inches square
>
> **Batting:** 3 inches square
>
> **Thick, white glue**

Shaker box: Heart-shaped, 4 inches across

Satin ribbon: Pink, ⅜x24 inches

Lace: 1x12 inches

Rattail cord: Pink, 10 inches

Acrylic paint: White

Flat paintbrush: 1 inch wide

Glue gun or thick, white glue

Scissors

Tapestry needle

2. Stitch

Follow the cross-stitching instructions given in Cross-Stitch Basics.

3. Finish

Finishing instructions for covering padded shapes are given in General Project Instructions. The following are additional instructions for this project.

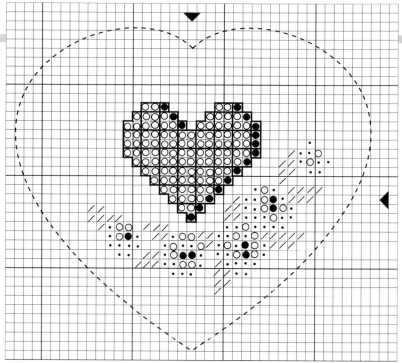

Bandbox Chart

Stitch Count: 27 x 21

- Paint the Shaker box, inside and out, with the white acrylic paint. Allow paint to dry.
- If you do not have a Stik 'N Puff heart, use the Cardboard and Batting Pattern, below, and cut the heart shape from the cardboard and the batting.
- Trace and cut out the Fabric Pattern, below. Place the pattern over the cross-stitched piece; hold up to the light to center it. Pin pattern to fabric; cut out fabric.
- Cover the Stik 'N Puff heart (or cardboard heart layered with batting) with the cross-stitched Aida fabric. Glue the lace to the back of the heart, letting about ½ inch extend beyond the edge of the heart. Start gluing at the V at the top of the heart and work your way around, pinching extra lace together at the bottom point; cut off excess lace when you reach the V again.
- Center the heart on the top of the painted box, and glue in place.
- Glue rattail cord around the heart where the padded shape meets the lace.
- Glue satin ribbon to the side of box lid.
- Tie the remaining satin ribbon in a simple bow and glue at the top of the padded heart.

Floss: (Symbol indicates color on chart.)

Symbol	Color name	DMC #	Anchor #
⋆	Light pink	818	49
○	Medium pink	957	55
●	Dark pink*	335	38
╱	Green	368	215

*Backstitch heart with dark pink.

Bandbox
Full-Size Cardboard
and Batting Pattern

Bandbox
Full-Size Fabric Pattern

79

For Easter

Bow-Tied Tulips,
page 83

Easter Love,
page 81

Classic Design,
page 84

Garden Tulips,
page 85

HAPPY
EASTER

Happy Easter,
page 82

Easter Love

1. Gather Materials

Aida fabric: 14 count, white, 4x5 inches
Stik 'N Puff: Two 2x2½-inch ovals
   (BANAR DESIGNS, Inc.) *or* Cardboard
   and Batting Pattern, below, and the
   following materials
   Cardboard: Heavyweight, 2x6 inches
   Batting: 2x6 inches
   Thick, white glue
Rattail cord: Pink, 12 inches
Fabric for backing: Pink, cotton moire or
   polished cotton, 4x5 inches
Glue gun or thick, white glue
Scissors
Tapestry needle

2. Stitch

Follow the cross-stitching instructions
given in Cross-Stitch Basics.

3. Finish

Finishing instructions for covering padded
shapes are given in General Project
Instructions. The following are additional
instructions for this project. Note: Each egg
is made from two ovals placed back to
back; one is covered with Aida fabric, the
other with plain, backing fabric.
■ If you do not have Stik 'N Puff ovals,
use the Cardboard and Batting Pattern,
below; cut the shape from cardboard and
batting.
■ Trace and cut out the Fabric Pattern,
right. Place the pattern over the cross-
stitched piece; hold up to the light to center
it. Pin pattern to fabric; cut out fabric.
■ Cover one Stik 'N Puff oval (or
cardboard oval layered with batting) with
the cross-stitched Aida fabric.
■ Cover the other Stik 'N Puff oval (or
cardboard oval layered with batting) with
the backing fabric.
■ Cut a 5-inch length of rattail cord to use
as a hanger. Fold cord in half; glue about

Easter Eggs
Full-Size Cardboard and Batting Pattern

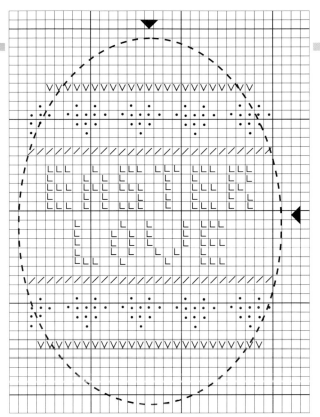

Easter Love Chart   Stitch Count: 26 x 29

Floss: (Symbol indicates color on chart.)

Symbol	Color name	DMC #	Anchor #
V	Blue	799	145
•	Pink	818	49
/	Green	912	205
L	Lavender	554	108

½ inch of the ends to the back of the Aida-
covered oval at the top.
■ Glue two ovals together, back to back.
■ Glue rattail cord around the ovals where
they meet, starting and ending at the top.

Making the Egg Tree

■ Use a paper-covered wire tree or natural
branch with many twigs (spray paint the
branch white).
■ Put floral foam in a small basket,
wedging it in tightly.
■ Insert the tree in the foam.
■ Put Easter "grass" in the top of the
basket to cover the foam.
■ Tie ⅜-inch pink satin ribbon into simple
bows on about 10 of the tree limbs (about
72 inches of ribbon total).
■ Hang stitched eggs from other limbs.
■ If the basket seems unstable, add weight
to the bottom.

Easter Eggs
Full-Size Fabric Pattern

Happy Easter

1. Gather Materials

Aida fabric: 14 count, white, 4x5 inches
Stik 'N Puff: Two 2x2½-inch ovals (BANAR DESIGNS, Inc.) *or* Cardboard and Batting Pattern on page 81 and the following materials:
    Cardboard: Heavyweight, 2x6 inches
    Batting: 2x6 inches
    Thick, white glue
Rattail cord: Light blue, 12 inches
Fabric for backing: Light blue, cotton moire or polished cotton, 4x5 inches

Glue gun or thick, white glue
Scissors
Tapestry needle

2. Stitch

Follow the cross-stitching instructions given in Cross-Stitch Basics.

3. Finish

Finishing instructions for covering padded shapes are given in General Project Instructions. The following are additional instructions for this project. Note: Each egg is made from two ovals placed back to back; one is covered with Aida fabric, the other with plain, backing fabric.

■ If you do not have Stik 'N Puff ovals, use the Cardboard and Batting Pattern on page 81; cut shape from cardboard and batting.

■ Trace and cut out the Fabric Pattern on page 81. Place the pattern over the cross-stitched piece; hold up to the light to center it. Pin pattern to fabric; cut out fabric.

■ Cover one Stik 'N Puff oval (or cardboard oval layered with batting) with the cross-stitched Aida fabric.

■ Cover the other Stik 'N Puff oval (or cardboard oval layered with batting) with the backing fabric.

■ Cut a 5-inch length of rattail cord to use as a hanger. Fold cord in half; glue about ½ inch of the ends to the back of the Aida-covered oval at the top.

■ Glue two ovals together, back to back.

■ Glue rattail cord around the ovals where they meet, starting and ending at the top.

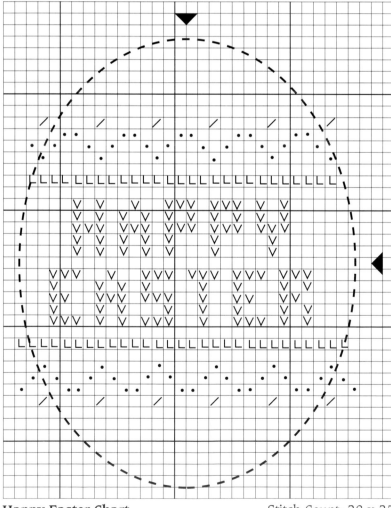

Happy Easter Chart   Stitch Count: 28 x 25

Floss: (Symbol indicates color on chart.)

Symbol	Color name	DMC #	Anchor #
V	Blue	799	145
•	Pink	818	49
L	Lavender	554	108
/	Green	912	205

Bow-Tied Tulips

1. Gather Materials

Aida fabric: 14 count, white, 4x5 inches
Stik 'N Puff: Two 2x2½-inch ovals
  (BANAR DESIGNS, Inc.) *or* Cardboard
  and Batting Pattern on page 81 and the
  following materials:
  Cardboard: Heavyweight, 2x6 inches
  Batting: 2x6 inches
  Thick, white glue
Rattail cord: Pink, 12 inches
Fabric for backing: Pink, cotton moire or
  polished cotton, 4x5 inches
Glue gun or thick, white glue
Scissors
Tapestry needle

2. Stitch

Follow the cross-stitching instructions
given in Cross-Stitch Basics.

3. Finish

Finishing instructions for covering padded
shapes are given in General Project
Instructions. The following are additional
instructions for this project. Note: Each egg
is made from two ovals placed back to
back; one is covered with Aida fabric, the
other with plain, backing fabric.
■ If you do not have Stik 'N Puff ovals,
use the Cardboard and Batting Pattern on
page 81; cut shape from cardboard and
batting.
■ Trace and cut out the Fabric Pattern on
page 81. Place the pattern over the cross-
stitched piece; hold up to the light to center
it. Pin pattern to fabric; cut out fabric.
■ Cover one Stik 'N Puff oval (or
cardboard oval layered with batting) with
the cross-stitched Aida fabric.
■ Cover one Stik 'N Puff oval (or
cardboard oval layered with batting) with
the backing fabric.

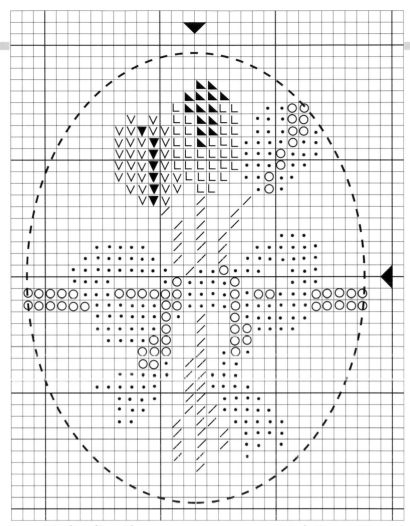

Bow-Tied Tulips Chart   Stitch Count: 30 x 34

Floss: (Symbol indicates color on chart.)

Symbol	Color name	DMC #	Anchor #
V	Blue	799	145
▼	Dark blue	798	146
L	Lavender	554	108
◤	Dark lavender	553	98
·	Pink	818	49
○	Dark pink	957	52
/	Green	912	205

■ Cut a 5-inch length of rattail cord to use
as a hanger. Fold cord in half; glue about
½ inch of the ends to the back of the Aida-
covered oval at the top.
■ Glue two ovals together, back to back.
■ Glue rattail cord around the ovals where
they meet, starting and ending at the top.

Classic Design

1. Gather Materials

Aida fabric: 14 count, white, 4x5 inches
Stik 'N Puff: Two 2x2½-inch ovals
(BANAR DESIGNS, Inc.) *or* Cardboard
and Batting Pattern on page 81 and the
following materials:
    Cardboard: Heavyweight, 2x6 inches
    Batting: 2x6 inches
    Thick, white glue

Rattail cord: Pink, 12 inches
Fabric for backing: Pink, cotton moire or
    polished cotton, 4x5 inches
Glue gun or thick, white glue
Scissors
Tapestry needle

2. Stitch

Follow the cross-stitching instructions
given in Cross-Stitch Basics.

3. Finish

Finishing instructions for covering padded
shapes are given in General Project
Instructions. The following are additional
instructions for this project. Note: Each egg
is made from two ovals placed back to
back; one is covered with Aida fabric, the
other with plain, backing fabric.
■ If you do not have Stik 'N Puff ovals,
use the Cardboard and Batting Pattern on
page 81; cut shape from cardboard and
batting.
■ Trace and cut out the Fabric Pattern on
page 81. Place the pattern over the cross-
stitched piece; hold up to the light to center
it. Pin pattern to fabric; cut out fabric.
■ Cover one Stik 'N Puff oval (or
cardboard oval layered with batting) with
the cross-stitched Aida fabric.
■ Cover the other Stik 'N Puff oval (or
cardboard oval layered with batting) with
the backing fabric.
■ Cut a 5-inch length of rattail cord to use
as a hanger. Fold cord in half; glue about
½ inch of the ends to the back of the Aida-
covered oval at the top.
■ Glue two ovals together, back to back.
■ Glue rattail cord around the ovals where
they meet, starting and ending at the top.

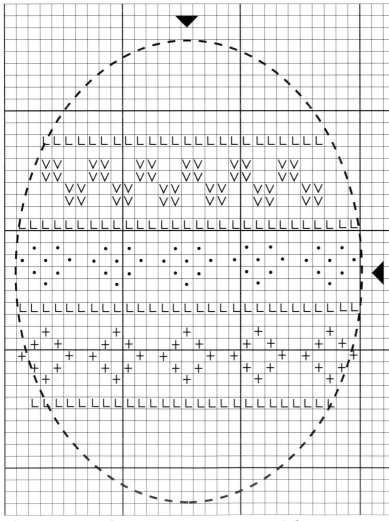

Classic Design Chart   Stitch Count: 29 x 23

Floss: (Symbol indicates color on chart.)

Symbol	Color name	DMC #	Anchor #
V	Blue	799	145
•	Pink	818	49
L	Lavender	554	108
+	Yellow	3078	292

Garden Tulips

1. Gather Materials

Aida fabric: 14 count, white, 4x5 inches
Stik 'N Puff: Two 2x2½-inch ovals
  (BANAR DESIGNS, Inc.) *or* Cardboard
  and Batting Pattern on page 81 and the
  following materials:
    Cardboard: Heavyweight, 2x6 inches
    Batting: 2x6 inches
    Thick, white glue
Rattail cord: Light blue, 12 inches
Fabric for backing: Light blue, cotton
  moire or polished cotton, 4x5 inches
Glue gun or thick, white glue
Scissors
Tapestry needle

2. Stitch

Follow the cross-stitching instructions
given in Cross-Stitch Basics.

3. Finish

Finishing instructions for covering padded
shapes are given in General Project
Instructions. The following are additional
instructions for this project. Note: Each egg
is made from two ovals placed back to
back; one is covered with Aida fabric, the
other with plain, backing fabric.
■ If you do not have Stik 'N Puff ovals,
use the Cardboard and Batting Pattern on
page 81 and cut the oval shape from the
cardboard and the batting.
■ Trace and cut out the Fabric Pattern on
page 81. Place the pattern over the cross-
stitched piece; hold up to the light to center
it. Pin pattern to fabric; cut out fabric.
■ Cover one Stik 'N Puff oval (or
cardboard oval layered with batting) with
the cross-stitched Aida fabric.
■ Cover the other Stik 'N Puff oval (or
cardboard oval layered with batting) with
the backing fabric.

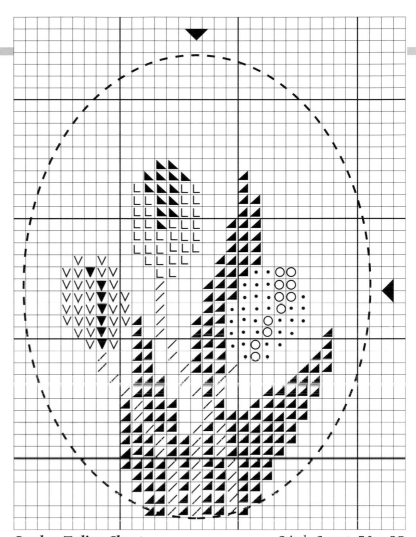

Garden Tulips Chart   Stitch Count: 30 x 23

Floss: (Symbol indicates color on chart.)

Symbol	Color name	DMC #	Anchor #
V	Blue	799	145
▼	Dark blue	798	146
L	Lavender	554	108
◣	Dark lavender	553	98
•	Pink	818	49
○	Dark pink	957	52
/	Green	912	205
◢	Dark green	910	229

■ Cut a 5-inch length of rattail cord to use
as a hanger. Fold cord in half; glue about
½ inch of the ends to the back of the Aida-
covered oval at the top.
■ Glue two ovals together, back to back.
■ Glue rattail cord around the ovals where
they meet, starting and ending at the top.

Flying the Flag

Bread Cover,
page 87

Napkin Rings,
page 87

Napkin Rings

1. Gather Materials

Ribband: 1½ inches wide, white with metallic gold scalloped edge, 6 inch length (for each napkin ring)
Scissors
Sewing machine, needle and thread, or fabric glue
Tapestry needle

2. Stitch

Follow the cross-stitching instructions in Cross-Stitch Basics.

3. Finish

■ After cross-stitching the design, cut ¼ inch of fabric off each end of a length of Ribband.
■ Bring the two ends of the Ribband together to form a napkin ring with the raw ends toward the inside.
■ Stitch or glue a ½-inch seam to attach the two ends.
■ Repeat for each napkin ring.

Bread Cover

1. Gather Materials

Bread cover: Premade, 18 inches square, white, Soft Touch, 100% Dacron (Charles Craft, #ST5503-6750), *or* the following materials:
    Even-weave fabric: 14 count, white, soft, washable fabric, 20 inches square
    Sewing machine or needle and thread
Scissors
Tapestry needle

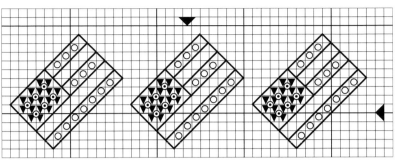

Napkin Ring Chart   Stitch Count: 41 x 13

Floss: (Symbol indicates color on chart.)

Symbol	Color name	DMC #	Anchor #
○	Red	321	47
▼	Blue	824	148
⊙	White*	Snow white	1
	Black*	310	403

*Backstitch flag with black. Stars are French knots done in white.

2. Stitch

Follow the cross-stitching instructions in Cross-Stitch Basics.

If you cannot locate the specified premade bread cover, cross-stitch the design on even-weave fabric 3 inches in from the edge and finish according to the following instructions.

Note: Don't let the diagonal appearance of the stitching confuse you. It is still done on the squares of the fabric, but the graph is designed to give the appearance of diagonal stitching. Hold one corner of the bread cover in your left hand; begin cross-stitching the design at the bottom of the chart, about 2 inches in from the fringed edge on each side.

3. Finish

Note: The premade bread cover requires no finishing. If you use an even-weave fabric, follow the instructions on page 88.

(continued)

Bread Cover
(continued)

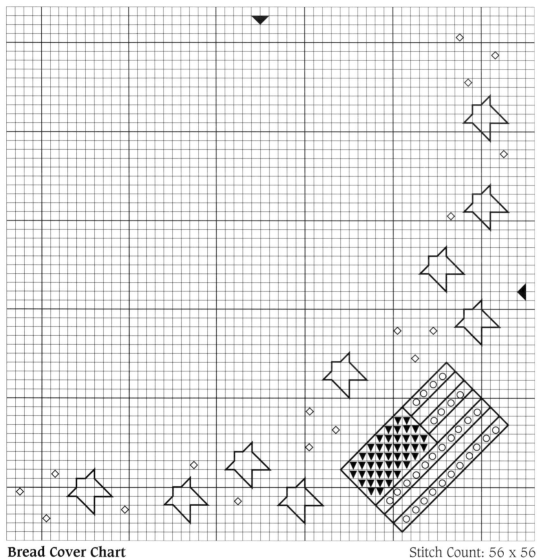

Bread Cover Chart

Stitch Count: 56 x 56

■ After cross-stitching the design, cut 1 inch of fabric off all four sides, leaving an 18-inch square of fabric.
■ Stitch ½ inch in from all the edges; fringe all four sides by pulling out the horizontal threads to the stitch line.

Floss: (Symbol indicates color on chart.)

Symbol	Color name	DMC #	Anchor #
○	Red	321	47
▼	Blue	824	148
◇	Yellow*	3078	292
◇	Metallic gold*	282	4640
	Black*	310	403

*Backstitch large stars with metallic gold and flag with black. Small stars around flag are French knots done in two strands of yellow and one strand of metallic gold.

Witch Way

Pumpkin Pin,
page 91

Witch Pin,
page 91

Ghost Pin,
page 90

Candy Tote,
page 92

Ghost Pin

1. Gather Materials

Perforated paper: 14 count, white,
  4 inches square (Yarn Tree Designs, Inc.)
Felt or decorative paper: White, 2 inches
  square
Tracing paper
Cellophane or masking tape
Pin back: 1¼ inches long
Thick, white glue
Glue gun or strong glue for metal
Tapestry needle
Scissors

2. Stitch

Follow the instructions for cross-stitching
given in Cross-Stitch Basics.

3. Finish

■ Trace the Perforated Paper Pattern,
below, onto tracing paper; cut out. Center
the tracing paper ghost shape over the
stitched paper using the rows of stitches on
the back of the head and under the arms as
a guide; the pattern should be at least one
hole bigger than the cross-stitched design.
Use tape to hold the pattern in place; cut
the ghost shape from the perforated paper,

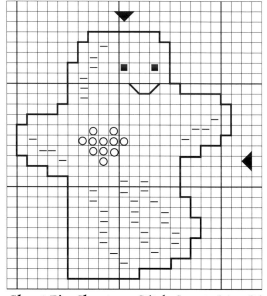

Ghost Pin Chart   Stitch Count: 21 x 24

Floss: (Symbol indicates color on chart.)

Symbol	Color name	DMC #	Anchor #
—	Gray	415	398
○	Pink	957	52
■	Black*	310	403
	*Backstitch mouth with black.		

cutting through both the tracing paper and
the perforated paper.
■ Use the Backing Pattern, left, to cut a
felt or decorative paper backing for the
design, cutting just inside the pattern lines.
It should be about ¹⁄₁₆ inch smaller than the
perforated paper shape. Spread an even
layer of white glue on the backing, and put
it on the back side of the cross-stitched
perforated paper.
■ Glue the pin back across the arms of the
ghost on the backing, using a glue gun or
other strong glue. Allow glue to dry.

Ghost Pin
Full-Size Perforated
Paper Pattern

Ghost Pin
Full-Size Backing
Pattern

Pumpkin Pin

1. Gather Materials

Perforated paper: 14 count, white,
  4 inches square (Yarn Tree Designs, Inc.)
Felt or decorative paper: White, 2 inches
  square
Pin back: 1¼ inches long
Thick, white glue
Glue gun or strong glue for metal
Tapestry needle
Scissors

2. Stitch

Follow the instructions for cross-stitching
given in Cross-Stitch Basics.

3. Finish

■ Carefully cut off the excess paper around
the cross-stitching, cutting through the first
row of holes just beyond the cross-
stitching (the first holes without thread
through them).
■ Use the pattern, right, to cut a felt or
decorative paper backing for the design.
It should be about ¹⁄₁₆ inch smaller than the
perforated paper shape. Spread an even
layer of white glue on the backing, and put
it on the back of the cross-stitched
perforated paper.
■ Glue the pin back horizontally in the
center of the back, using a glue gun or
other strong glue. Allow glue to dry.

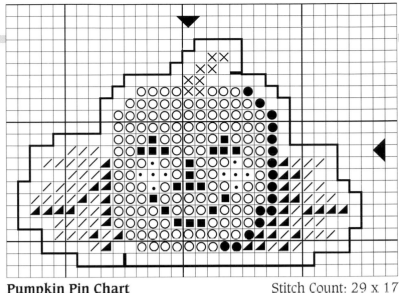

Pumpkin Pin Chart   Stitch Count: 29 x 17

Floss: (Symbol indicates color on chart.)

Symbol	Color name	DMC #	Anchor #
○	Light orange	740	316
●	Dark orange	920	339
■	Black	310	403
×	Brown	433	371
•	Pink	957	52
⁄	Light green	912	205
◢	Dark green	910	229

Pumpkin Pin
Full-Size Pattern

Witch Pin

1. Gather Materials

Perforated paper: 14 count, white,
  4 inches square (Yarn Tree Designs, Inc.)
Felt or decorative paper: White, 2 inches
  square
Pin back: 1¼ inches long
Round toothpick
Thick, white glue
Glue gun or strong glue for metal
Tapestry needle
Scissors   *(continued)*

Witch Pin
(continued)

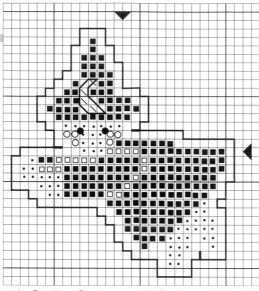

Witch Pin Chart   Stitch Count: 24 x 27

Floss: (Symbol indicates color on chart.)

Symbol	Color name	DMC #	Anchor #
■	Black	310	403
•	Flesh	948	6
○	Pink	957	52
\	Yellow	3078	300
□	Gray	414	235

Witch Pin
Full-Size Pattern

2. Stitch

Follow the instructions for cross-stitching given in Cross-Stitch Basics.

3. Finish

■ Carefully cut off the excess paper around the cross-stitching, cutting through the first row of holes just beyond the cross-stitching (the first holes without thread through them).

■ Cut the pointed ends off the toothpick to make the broom handle. Glue toothpick to back of perforated paper with about ¼ inch extending above witch's hand at an angle (see photo, page 89).

■ Make the broom straw using eight strands of yellow floss 2 inches long. Fold the floss in half; tie yellow floss around the folded strands about ¼ inch down from the fold. Glue fold near the bottom end of the broom handle.

■ Use the pattern, below left, to cut a felt or decorative paper backing for the design. It should be about ⅟₁₆ inch smaller than the perforated paper shape. Spread an even layer of white glue on the backing, and put it on the back of the cross-stitched perforated paper.

■ Glue the pin back horizontally in the center of the back, using a glue gun or other strong glue. Allow glue to dry.

Candy Tote

1. Gather Materials

Burlap: Approximately 7 count, 15x32 inches (James Thompson)
Twine: Jute or other heavy cord, 64 inches
Sewing machine or needle and thread
Iron
Tapestry needle
Scissors

2. Stitch

Fold the burlap in half to form a 15x16-inch rectangle; press the fold with an iron to crease it. Unfold the fabric, and cross-stitch the design in the center of the upper half of the burlap (with the raw edge at the top and the fold at the bottom). Follow the instructions for cross-stitching over two threads given in Cross-Stitch Basics.

3. Finish

■ After cross-stitching the design, fold each short end toward the front ¼ inch; stitch. To form a casing for the twine, fold each short end toward the front 1 inch and stitch on the seamed edge; the ends should remain open.

■ Fold the burlap in half along the pressed fold with the cross-stitched design inside. Stitch ½-inch seams along each side; leave the top 1 inch unstitched at the casing.

■ Turn the bag right side out.

■ Cut the twine in half to make handles. Run one piece of the twine through the casing at the top, beginning and ending on the right side (attach a large safety pin to the twine to help thread it through the pocket). Tie the ends of twine together in a strong knot. Run the other piece of twine through the casing, beginning and ending on the left side; tie its ends together in a knot.

Floss: (Symbol indicates color on chart.)

Symbol	Color name	DMC #	Anchor #
○	Orange	971	316
■	Black	310	403
I	White	Snow white	1
◇	Gold	742	303

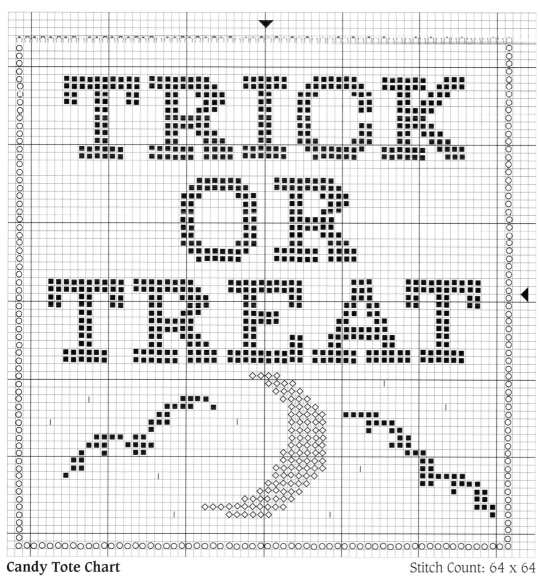

Candy Tote Chart

Stitch Count: 64 x 64

Bountiful Harvest

Napkins,
page 96

Place Mats,
page 95

Place Mats

1. Gather Materials

Place mats: Premade, 13x18 inches, white, Royal Classic (Charles Craft, #RC4851-6750), *or* washable even-weave fabric, 14 count, white, 15x20 inches (for each place mat), and the following materials:

Sewing machine or needle and thread
Scissors
Tapestry needle

2. Stitch

Follow the cross-stitching instructions in Cross-Stitch Basics. The design is cross-stitched 1 inch in from the edge of the place mat. *(continued)*

Floss: (Symbol indicates color on chart.)

Symbol	Color name	DMC #	Anchor #
ı	Beige	437	368
+	Light brown	435	369
✕	Medium brown	975	370
✳	Dark brown	433	371
◱	Gray	414	235
■	Black	310	403
╲	Light yellow	677	886
—	Medium yellow	744	302
•	Pink	957	52
○	Red	321	47
●	Dark red	498	20
◇	Medium orange	722	304
⬖	Dark orange	740	316
L	Light lavender	211	342
◣	Medium lavender	553	98
◣	Dark lavender	208	110
╱	Light green	912	205
◢	Dark green	910	229

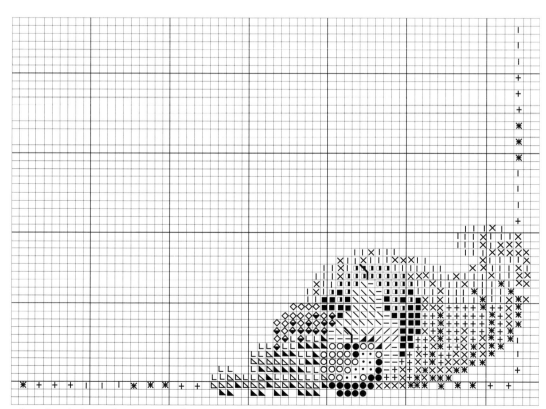

Thanksgiving Place Mat Chart   Stitch Count: 40 x 22
(Continue the border stitches around the entire place mat, rotating the colors.)

Place Mats
(continued)

If you cannot locate the premade place mats, cross-stitch the design 2 inches in from the edge of the 15x20-inch piece of even-weave fabric and finish according to the following instructions.

3. Finish

Note: Premade place mats require no finishing. If you use an even-weave fabric, follow the instructions below.
■ After cross-stitching the design, cut 1 inch of fabric off all four sides, leaving a 13x18-inch rectangle of fabric.
■ Stitch ½ inch in from all the edges; fringe all four sides to the stitch line by pulling out the horizontal threads.
■ Repeat for each place mat.

Napkins

1. Gather Materials

Napkins: Premade, 15 inches square, white, Royal Classic (Charles Craft, #RC4852-6750), *or* washable even-weave fabric, 14 count, white, 17 inches square (for each napkin), and the following materials
   Sewing machine or needle and thread
Scissors
Tapestry needle

2. Stitch

Follow cross-stitching instructions in Cross-Stitch Basics. The design is cross-stitched 1 inch in from edge of napkin. If you cannot locate premade napkins, cross-stitch design 2 inches in from edge of a 17-inch square of even-weave fabric; finish according to the following instructions.

3. Finish

Note: Premade napkins require no finishing. If you use an even-weave fabric, follow the instructions below.
■ After cross-stitching the design, cut 1 inch of fabric off all four sides, leaving a 15-inch square of fabric.
■ Stitch ½ inch in from all the edges; fringe all four sides to the stitch line by pulling out the horizontal threads.
■ Repeat for each napkin.

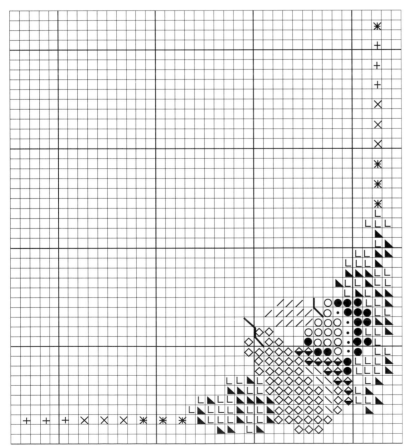

Napkin Chart   Stitch Count: 38 x 42
(Continue the border stitches around the entire napkin, rotating the colors.)

Floss: (Symbol indicates color on chart.)

Symbol	Color name	DMC #	Anchor #
+	Light brown	435	369
×	Medium brown	975	370
✳	Dark brown	433	371
╲	Light yellow	677	886
◇	Medium yellow	744	302
◆	Dark yellow	783	306
•	Pink	957	52
○	Red	321	47
●	Dark red	498	20
L	Light lavender	211	342
◣	Dark lavender	208	110
╱	Dark green	910	229

For Christmas

Holiday Keepsakes

Pillow,
page 102

Welcome Mat,
page 101

Santa Cones,
page 98

Santa Cones

1. Gather Materials

Aida fabric: 14 count, red (Charles Craft)
  Fat Santa: 9x6 inches
  Tall Santa: 6x9 inches
  Short Santa: 6x5 inches

Fiberfill: Large handful for each Santa
Sewing needle and red thread
Strong fabric glue or sewing machine
Scissors
Tapestry needle

2. Stitch

Follow the cross-stitching instructions given in Cross-Stitch Basics.

3. Finish

■ After cross-stitching the design, hold the cross-stitched fabric up to the light; center the corresponding Santa Cone pattern on page 100 or 101 over the design. Pin in place; cut out. Place the pattern on unstitched Aida fabric; pin in place and cut out. Place the plain Aida fabric on work surface; lay the cross-stitched Aida over it, wrong side up (design side down); pin together. Glue or stitch a ½-inch seam around the shape, leaving the bottom open.

■ Stitch a ¼-inch hem in the bottom edges, folding the fabric to the outside.

■ Turn right side out. Run a line of basting stitches around the bottom edge; leave 6-inch tails to gather bottom closed later.

■ Stuff Santa with fiberfill, using a pencil or other tool to push the batting firmly into the point at the top of the head. Stop stuffing about ½ inch from the bottom.

■ Pull the gathering threads to close the bottom, pushing the excess fabric into the opening as you gather; tie securely.

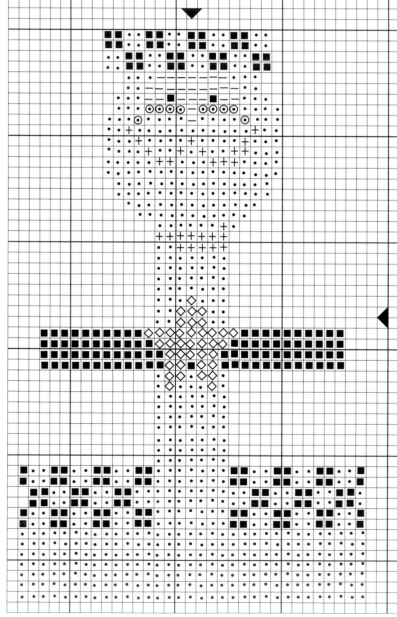

Fat Santa Cone Chart

Stitch Count: 33 x 54

Floss: (Symbol indicates color on chart.)

Symbol	Color name	DMC #	Anchor #
•	White	Snow white	1
—	Flesh	754	6
■	Black	310	403
⊙	Pink	957	52
+	Gray	415	398
◇	Gold	743	302

Note: These Santa Cones are versatile decorations. If you want them to stand up on a mantle, insert weights (such as washers) in the bottom before gathering. You can stand them among the greens in a centerpiece or glue them securely on a wreath. To make ornaments, you can run a gold thread through the top of the cone.

(continued)

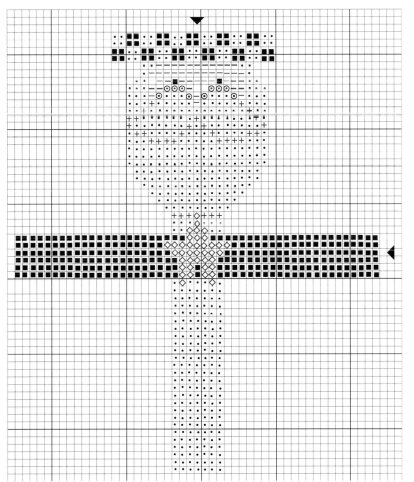

Short Santa Cone Chart

Stitch Count: 49 x 59

Floss: (Symbol indicates color on chart.)

Symbol	Color name	DMC #	Anchor #
•	White	Snow white	1
—	Flesh	754	6
■	Black	310	403
⊙	Pink	957	52
+	Gray	415	398
◇	Gold	743	302

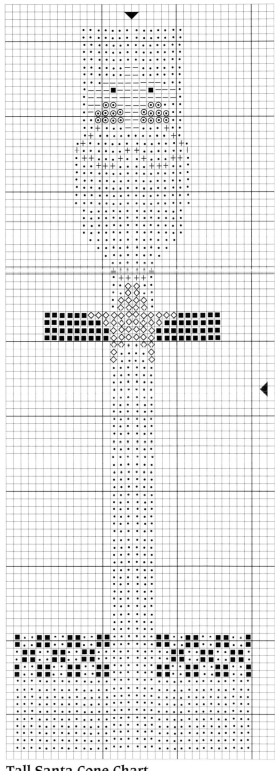

Tall Santa Cone Chart
Stitch Count: 32 x 97

Santa Cones
(continued)

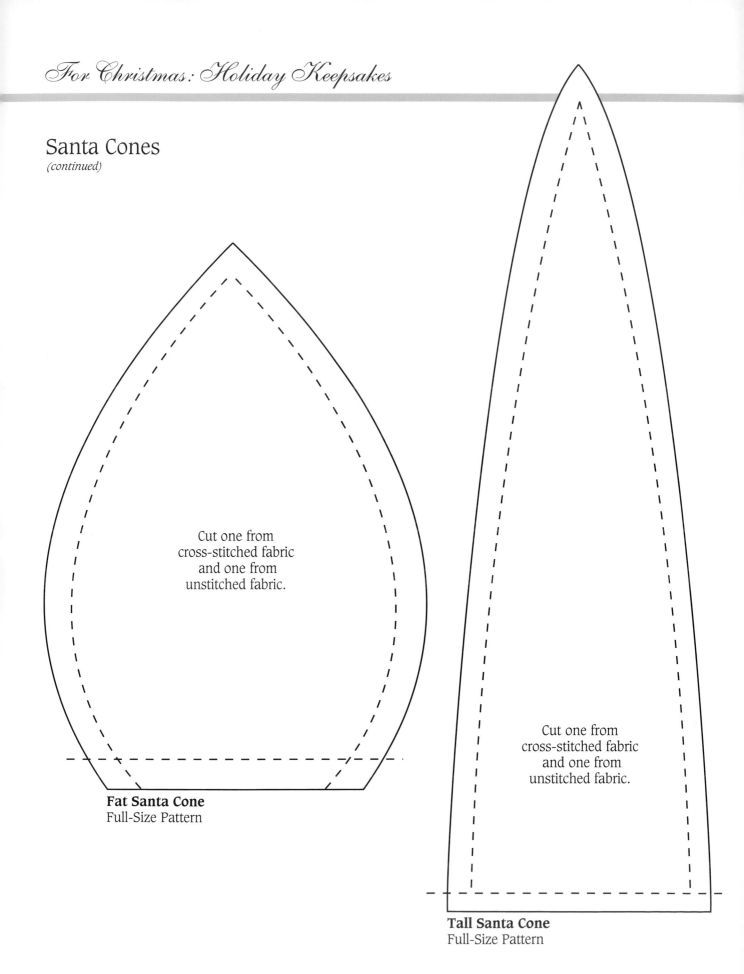

Cut one from
cross-stitched fabric
and one from
unstitched fabric.

Fat Santa Cone
Full-Size Pattern

Cut one from
cross-stitched fabric
and one from
unstitched fabric.

Tall Santa Cone
Full-Size Pattern

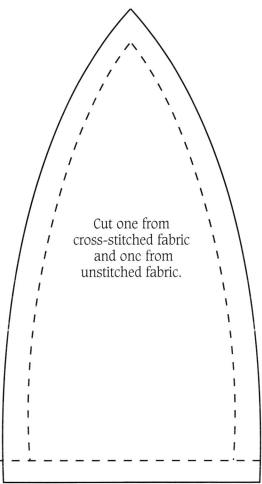

Cut one from cross-stitched fabric and one from unstitched fabric.

Short Santa Cone
Full-Size Pattern

Welcome Mat

1. Gather Materials

Grass mat: Half circle, 17x30 inches
Fabric: Cotton or 50/50 cotton/polyester blend, 45 inches wide (see chart, bottom right, for colors and yardage)
Needle: Large metal or plastic (as used for plastic canvas work)
Scissors

2. Stitch

Note: Wash and dry fabric. Cut into 1½-inch-wide strips, cutting across the width of the fabric (selvage to selvage).
■ Center the design on the mat, using the center tree as a guide.

■ Using the strips of fabric as your floss and the spaces in the mat as holes, make half cross-stitches following the instructions given in Cross-Stitch Basics. Angle your half cross-stitches from lower left to upper right. As you thread your needle and pull the fabric through the holes in the mat, the fabric will fold automatically; keep the printed side out.
■ Leave about 3 inches of fabric on the back of the mat each time you start a new fabric strip; catch this end under the next several half cross-stitches, just as you would with floss. To end a strip, run about 3 inches under several half cross-stitches on the back; cut off excess fabric. Start new strips as needed.
■ Overcast the edges of the mat with red fabric strips: From the back, come up through a hole next to the edge, take the strip over the edge, and come up from the back again in the next hole (see photo, page 97).

3. Finish

No finishing is required, but you may want to spray the finished mat with a fabric protector.

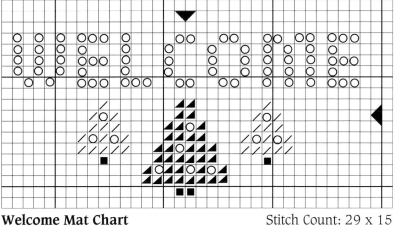

Welcome Mat Chart   Stitch Count: 29 x 15

Fabric: (Symbol indicates color on chart.)

Symbol	Fabric Color	Yardage
○	Red solid	1 yard
╱	Light green plaid	⅛ yard
◢	Dark green solid	⅛ yard
■	Black print	⅛ yard

Pillow

1. Gather Materials

Pillow: Premade with 7-count even-weave front, 11 inches square plus 2½-inch gathered ruffle (Adam Originals), *or* the following materials:
  Even-weave fabric: 7 count, natural, 14 inches square (such as Klostern by Zweigart)
  Fabric for backing: Coordinating color, cotton or cotton/polyester, 12 inches square
  Gathered ruffle: Red and green plaid, 3x48 inches
  Straight pins
  Sewing machine, needle and thread, or washable fabric glue
Pillow form: 11 inches square
Tapestry needle
Scissors

2. Stitch

Unzip the premade pillow and reach inside to cross-stitch the design. Follow the cross-stitching instructions given in Cross-Stitch Basics. Use six strands of floss for all stitching.

If you cannot locate a pillow premade with an even-weave front, cross-stitch the design in the center of the 14-inch-square even-weave fabric and finish according to the following instructions.

3. Finish

Note: The pillow premade with even-weave front requires no finishing. Just insert pillow form after cross-stitching the design and zip shut. If you are making a pillow, follow the instructions below.

■ After cross-stitching the design on the even-weave fabric, cut off 1 inch of the fabric on all four sides, leaving a 12-inch square of stitched fabric.

■ Place the cross-stitched, even-weave front, design side up, on your work surface.

■ Place the ruffle on top with the gathered edge at the raw edge of the even-weave fabric and the finished edge toward the inside; pin in place as you go. Pinch together extra ruffle at the corners to avoid puckering when the pillow is turned. When you return to the starting point, leave a ½-inch overlap and cut off the excess. Stitch the two ends of the ruffle together.

■ Place the 12-inch-square piece of cotton backing on top of the ruffle with right side down; pin.

■ When all layers are assembled, stitch pillow together with ½-inch seams, leaving one side open for turning. Remove pins, and turn the pillow right side out through the open side.

■ Insert pillow form. Whipstitch the open side closed, making sure to fold in about ½ inch of fabric from the front and back of the pillow and to catch the edge of the ruffle between them.

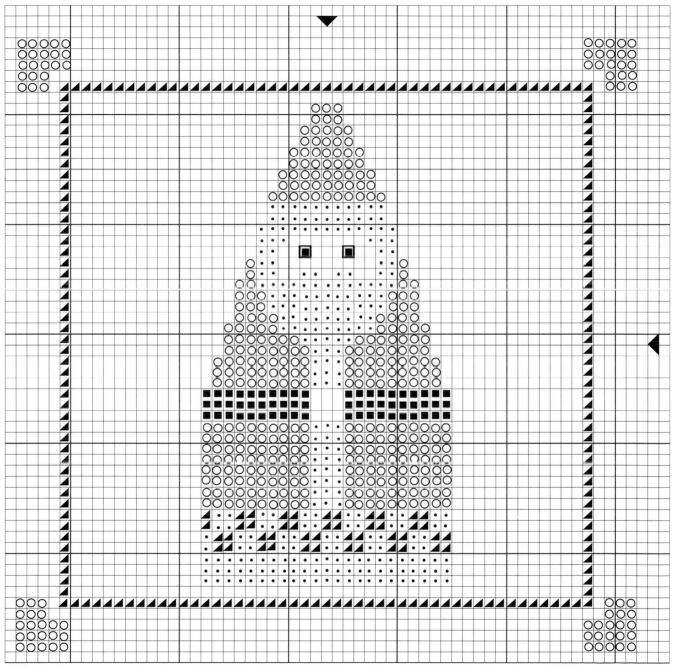

Pillow Chart

Stitch Count: 57 x 56

Floss: (Symbol indicates color on chart.)

Symbol	Color name	DMC#	Anchor#
◤	Dark green	319	218
○	Medium red	321	19
•	White	Snow white	1
■	Black*	310	403

*Backstitch around eyes with black.

Napkin Rings

1. Gather Materials

Anne cloth: White, 3x6½ inches
(for each napkin)
Scissors
Thick, white glue
Tapestry needle

2. Stitch

Follow the cross-stitching instructions for stitching over two threads given in Cross-Stitch Basics. Cross-stitch the design in the center of the fabric, making sure there are no vertical or horizontal woven lines to interfere with the design.

3. Finish

■ After cross-stitching the design, fold back the edges ½ inch. Press the folds with an iron to crease.
■ Trim excess fabric away at the corners, cutting at a 45-degree angle.
■ Unfold the fabric, and apply an even coat of glue to the back of each flap; smooth the flaps firmly back into place and allow to dry. As an alternative to gluing, you can stitch the flaps down.
■ Bring the two ends of the napkin ring together; overlap ¼ inch and glue or stitch together.
■ Repeat for each napkin ring.

Napkin Rings, page 104

Place Mats page 105

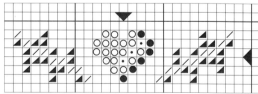

Napkin Ring Chart   Stitch Count: 25 x 6

Floss: (Symbol indicates color on chart.)

Symbol	Color Name	DMC #	Anchor #
•	Pink	957	55
○	Medium Red	321	19
●	Dark Red	498	20
/	Medium green	910	230
◢	Dark green	319	218

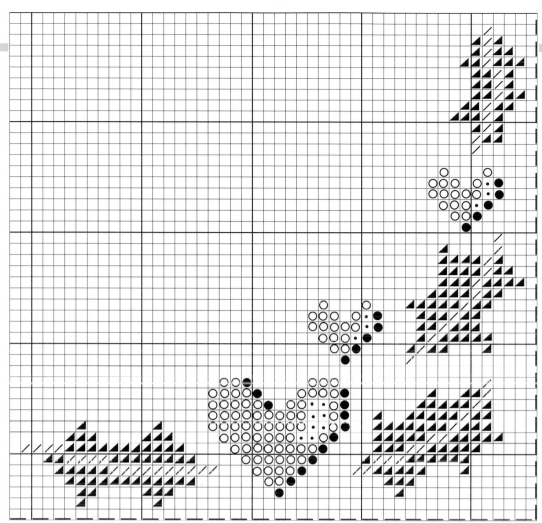

Place Mat Chart

Stitch Count: 46 x 43

Place Mats

1. Gather Materials

Anne cloth: White, 17x23 inches
including 2-inch-wide fringe (for each
place mat)
Scissors
Sewing machine or needle and thread
Tapestry needle

2. Stitch

Follow the cross-stitching instructions for
stitching over two threads given in Cross-
Stitch Basics. The design is cross-stitched
in the lower right corner of the fabric,
inside the vertical and horizontal woven
lines (see photo, page 104, and the chart,
above.)

Floss: (Symbol indicates color on chart.)

Symbol	Color name	DMC#	Anchor#
•	Pink	957	55
○	Medium Red	321	19
●	Dark Red	498	20
/	Medium green	910	230
◢	Dark green	319	218

3. Finish

■After cross-stitching the design, stitch on
the horizontal and vertical lines of the
design near the edges of the place mat.
■Fringe all four sides to the stitching line
(in about 2 inches) by pulling out the
horizontal threads.
■ Repeat for each place mat.

Gifts for the Home

❖ ❖ ❖

Welcome a new neighbor or remember a gracious host with a custom-made decoration for the home. You'll find everything from charming kitchen place mats, to a precious hand towel for the bath, to an inviting Home Sweet Home sampler.

Bubbling Delights

Banded Basket,
page 109

Privacy Sign,
page 108

Hand Towel,
page 111

DO NOT DISTURB

Privacy Sign

1. Gather Materials

Aida fabric: 14 count, white, 7 inches square
Cardboard: Heavyweight, 5 inches square
Batting: 4 inches square
Felt: White, 5 inches square
Rattail cord: Light blue, 30 inches
Cluny lace: Gathered, white, 1x20 inches
Glue gun or thick, white glue
Scissors
Tapestry needle

2. Stitch

Follow the cross-stitching instructions given in Cross-Stitch Basics.

3. Finish

Finishing instructions for covering padded shapes are given in General Project Instructions. The following are additional instructions for this project.

■ Using the Privacy Sign pattern on page 109, cut the arched shape from the cardboard, batting, and felt. Glue the batting to the cardboard.
■ Cut the cross-stitched Aida fabric about 1 inch larger than the pattern with the word "Disturb" about 1½ inches above the bottom edge.
■ Cover the batting-covered cardboard with the cross-stitched Aida fabric (see Padded Shapes, page 166).
■ Glue lace to the back of the arched shape, starting at the bottom, with about ¾ inch extending out around the covered shape. At the corners, pinch more of the lace together as you glue it down in order to get enough lace to turn the corner attractively.
■ Form a hanger by gluing the ends of a 12-inch length of rattail cord about 3 inches apart at the top of the arch.
■ Glue rattail cord around the arch where the padded shape meets the lace.
■ Apply an even layer of glue to the felt and press onto the back of the covered shape. Allow glue to dry.

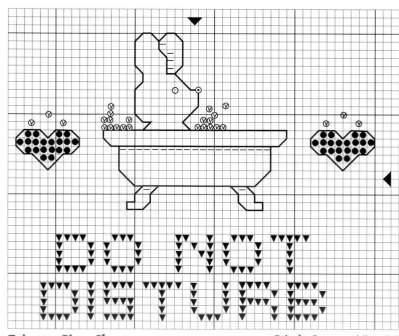

Privacy Sign Chart   Stitch Count: 45 x 36

Floss: (Symbol indicates color on chart.)

Symbol	Color name	DMC #	Anchor #
ⓥ	Light blue*	932	920
▼	Medium blue	798	146
—	Medium gray	414	235
⊙	Light pink*	776	73
●	Medium pink	957	52
	Black*	310	403

*Backstitching is done with black. Eye is French knot done in black. Bubbles are French knots done in light blue; nose is French knot done in light pink.

Privacy Sign
Full-Size Pattern

Banded Basket

1. Gather Materials

Ribband: 14 count, white Aida, light blue
scalloped edge, 1¾x34 inches, *or* the
following materials:
  Aida fabric: 14 count, white, 4x40
  inches
  Ribbon: ¼x72 inches, *or* lace: ½x72
  inches
  Washable fabric glue
Basket: 6 inches wide, 8 inches long,
  4½ inches high
Tapestry needle
Iron

Scissors
Thick, white glue
**Sewing machine or needle and thread
  (optional)**

2. Stitch

Follow the cross-stitching instructions
given in Cross-Stitch Basics.

If you cannot locate Ribband, cross-stitch
the design on Aida fabric and finish
according to the following instructions.

(continued)

Banded Basket

(continued)

3. Finish

Measurements assume a basket of the dimensions given above; adjust as necessary for smaller or larger baskets.

■ After cross-stitching the design on Ribband, cut 1 inch off only the ends. If stitching is done on Aida fabric, cut 1 inch off all four sides.

■ Fold back the Ribband or Aida fabric ½ inch on each end of the cross-stitched design. Press the folds with an iron to crease.

■ Hemstitch the folded ends or glue in place. To glue, unfold the fabric, and apply an even coat of glue to each flap; smooth the flaps firmly into place and allow to dry.

■ Apply fabric glue to the entire back of the cross-stitched band; press firmly in place on the basket, just beneath the top rim. Start and end at the back of the basket.

■ If using Aida, glue ribbon or lace over the raw edges of the fabric at the top and bottom of the band (where the Ribband has scalloped edges), starting and ending at the back of the basket.

Floss: (Symbol indicates color on chart.)

Symbol	Color name	DMC #	Anchor #
/	Medium green	910	229
●	Medium pink	957	52
⊘	Light blue*	932	920
	Black*	310	403

*Backstitching with black. Bubbles are French knots done in light blue.

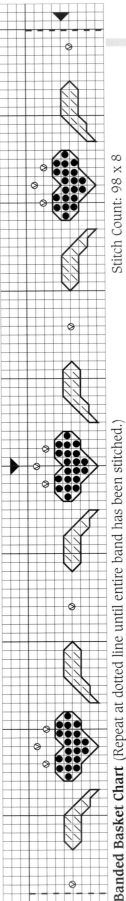

Stitch Count: 98 x 8

Banded Basket Chart (Repeat at dotted line until entire band has been stitched.)

Hand Towel

1. Gather Materials

Towel: Premade, 15x24 inches, with a 3-inch-wide even-weave fabric insert woven in horizontally (Charles Craft, No. TT6623-0900), *or* plain towel without even-weave band and the following materials:

    Aida fabric: 14 count, white, 6x18 inches, *or* Ribband: 2½x18 inches

    Washable ribbon: Light blue, ¼x32 inches (if not using Ribband)

    Washable fabric glue

    Sewing machine or needle and thread

Scissors

Tapestry needle

Iron

2. Stitch

Cross-stitch the design on the band of the premade towel. Follow the cross-stitching instructions given in Cross-Stitch Basics.

If you cannot locate a towel premade with an even-weave insert, cross-stitch the design on Aida fabric or Ribband, and finish according to the following instructions.

3. Finish

Note: The premade towel requires no finishing. If you are adding a cross-stitched panel to a plain towel, follow the instructions below.

■ After cross-stitching the design on Aida, cut off 1 inch of the fabric from all four sides, leaving a 4x16-inch piece of cross-stitched fabric. If using Ribband, cut 1 inch off only the ends.

■ Fold back the Aida fabric ½ inch on all four sides of the cross-stitched design. Press the folds with an iron to crease. If using Ribband, fold back only the ends and press.

■ Trim excess Aida fabric away at the corners, cutting at a 45-degree angle.

■ Hemstitch the flaps in place with a needle and thread.

■ Sew the washable ribbon on each of the long edges of the Aida with half on the fabric and half off; fold each end back ½ inch.

■ Sew the cross-stitched fabric to the towel with a sewing machine or needle and thread.

Floss: (Symbol indicates color on chart.)

Symbol	Color name	DMC #	Anchor #
ⓥ	Light blue*	932	920
⊙	Light pink*	776	73
—	Gray	414	235
●	Medium pink	957	52
	Black*	310	403

*Backstitch with black. Eye is French knot done in black. Bubbles are French knots done in light blue; nose is French knot done in light pink.

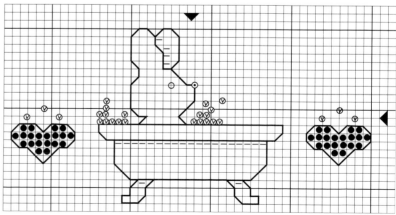

Hand Towel Chart

Stitch Count: 45 x 22

Fruits of Our Labors

Jar Top,
page 116

Recipe Box,
page 117

Recipes

Pot Holder,
page 113

Oven Mitt,
page 114

Pot Holder

Floss: (Symbol indicates color on chart.)

Symbol	Color name	DMC #	Anchor #
■	Black	310	403
╱	Light green	504	875
◿	Medium green	502	877
◢	Dark green	319	218
·	Pink	818	49
○	Medium red	321	47
●	Dark red	498	20
V	Light blue	3761	160

1. Gather Materials

Potholder: Premade, ecru, quilted,
8 inches square, with 5½x7-inch Aida
fabric insert (Charles Craft, No. PH6201),
or plain pot holder without Aida front
and the following materials:
   Aida fabric: 14 count, white,
     8 inches square
   Washable ribbon or lace:
     Coordinating color, 24 inches
     (optional, for trim)
   **Sewing machine or needle and
     white thread**
   Iron
Scissors
Tapestry needle   *(continued)*

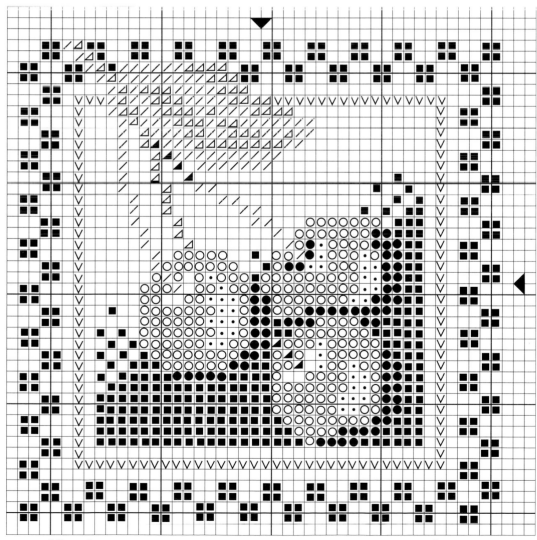

Pot Holder Chart   Stitch Count: 44 x 44

Pot Holder
(continued)

2. Stitch

Cross-stitch the design on the premade pot holder. Follow the cross-stitching instructions given in Cross-Stitch Basics.

If you cannot locate a pot holder premade with an Aida insert, cross-stitch the design on Aida fabric and finish according to the following instructions.

3. Finish

Note: The premade pot holder requires no finishing. If you are adding a cross-stitched front to a plain pot holder, follow the instructions below.

■ After cross-stitching the design on Aida, cut off 1 inch of the fabric from all four sides, leaving a 6-inch square piece of cross-stitched fabric.

■ Fold back the Aida fabric ½ inch on all four sides of the cross-stitched design. Press the folds with an iron to crease.

■ Trim excess Aida fabric away at the corners, cutting at a 45-degree angle.

■ Stitch the flaps in place with a machine or hemstitch by hand.

■ Center cross-stitched piece on the pot holder and sew in place on the front of the pot holder.

■ To give a more finished appearance, you can add a border of washable ribbon or lace around the Aida. Sew the lace or ribbon on each of the edges of the Aida square with about ⅛ inch on the fabric and the rest extending onto the pot holder.

Oven Mitt

1. Gather Materials

Oven mitt: Premade, ecru, quilted, with 4x8-inch Aida fabric insert (Charles Craft, No. OM6301), *or* plain oven mitt without Aida front and the following materials:
  Aida fabric: 14 count, white, 7 inches square
  Washable ribbon or lace: Coordinating color, 18 inches (optional, for trim)
  Sewing machine or needle and white thread
  Iron
Scissors
Tapestry needle

2. Stitch

Cross-stitch the design toward one side of the Aida band on the premade oven mitt. Follow the cross-stitching instructions given in Cross-Stitch Basics.

If you cannot locate an oven mitt premade with an Aida insert, cross-stitch the design on Aida fabric and finish according to the following instructions.

3. Finish

Note: The premade oven mitt requires no finishing. If you are adding a cross-stitched design to a plain oven mitt, follow the instructions below.

■ After cross-stitching the design on Aida, cut off 1 inch of the fabric from all four sides, leaving a 5-inch square of cross-stitched fabric.

■ Fold back the Aida fabric ½ inch on all four sides of the cross-stitched design. Press the folds with an iron to crease.

■ Trim excess Aida fabric away at the corners, cutting at a 45-degree angle.

■ Stitch the flaps in place near the fold with a machine or hemstitch by hand.
■ Sew the cross-stitched Aida fabric to the oven mitt about 1 inch from the open end and 1 inch from one side.
■ To give a more finished appearance, you can add a border of washable ribbon or lace around the Aida. Sew the lace or ribbon to each side of the Aida square with about ⅛ inch on the fabric and the rest extending onto the oven mitt.

Floss: (Symbol indicates color on chart.)

Symbol	Color name	DMC #	Anchor #
■	Black	310	403
/	Light green	504	875
◿	Medium green	502	877
◢	Dark green	319	218
○	Medium red	321	47
●	Dark red	814	45
V	Light blue	3761	160
×	Brown	975	370

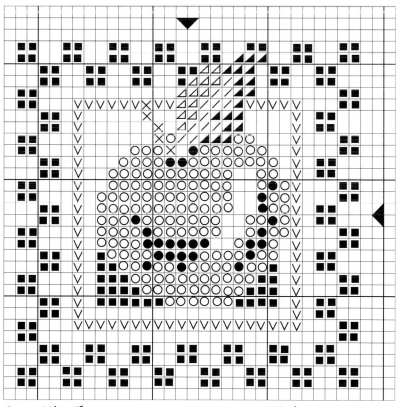

Oven Mitt Chart

Stitch Count: 30 x 30

Jar Top

1. Gather Materials

Aida fabric: 14 count, ecru, 6 inches square

Stik 'N Puff: One 2½-inch round (BANAR DESIGNS, Inc.), *or* Cardboard and Batting Pattern on page 117, and the following materials:

   Cardboard: Heavyweight, 3 inches square

   Batting: 3 inches square

Eyelet lace: Ecru, 1x12 inches

Satin ribbon: Red, ⅜x24 inches

Jar with lid: Approximately 2½ inches in diameter

Thick, white glue and/or glue gun
Scissors
Tapestry needle

2. Stitch

Follow the cross-stitching instructions given in Cross-Stitch Basics.

3. Finish

Finishing instructions for covering padded shapes are given in General Project Instructions. The following are additional instructions for this project.

■ Cover the padded circle with the cross-stitched Aida fabric.

■ Glue padded Aida onto top of jar lid.

■ Glue eyelet lace around neck of jar (see photo, page 112).

■ Glue red ribbon over lace, starting with center of ribbon at top of design and tying the ends together in a bow at the bottom.

Floss: (Symbol indicates color on chart.)

Symbol	Color Name	DMC #	Anchor #
V	Medium blue	3761	160
■	Black	310	403
/	Light green	504	875
◢	Medium green	502	877
○	Medium red	321	47
●	Dark red	814	45

Jar Top Chart   Stitch Count: 36 x 25

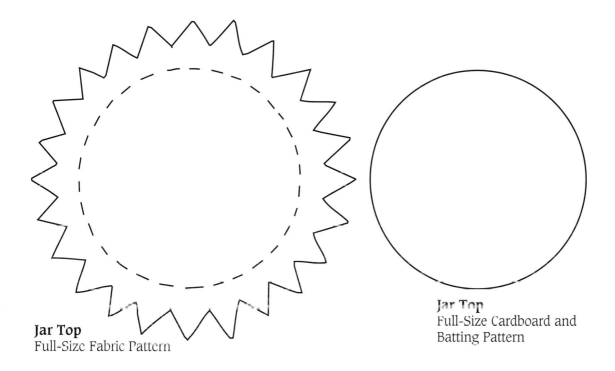

Jar Top
Full-Size Fabric Pattern

Jar Top
Full-Size Cardboard and
Batting Pattern

Recipe Box

1. Gather Materials

Aida fabric: 14 count, ecru, 7x9 inches
Cardboard: Heavyweight, 3½x5 inches
Batting: 3½x5 inches
Recipe box: Whitewashed wood,
   5x7 inches
Thick, white glue
Rattail cord: Red, 18 inches
Stencil: Checked design (optional)
Paint: Black acrylic (optional)
Stencil brush (optional)
Scissors
Tapestry needle

2. Stitch

Follow the cross-stitching instructions
given in Cross-Stitch Basics.

3. Finish

Finishing instructions for covering padded
shapes are given in General Project
Instructions. The following are additional
instructions for this project.

■ If you want to stencil the checked design
on the box, do so before attaching the
cross-stitched piece. Tape the stencil in
place on the box front and top. For best
coverage, wipe almost all the paint off the
stencil brush onto paper towels, and use
circular brush motions while stenciling.
Allow paint to dry.

■ After cross-stitching the design on Aida,
cut off 1 inch of the fabric from all four
sides, leaving a 5x7-inch rectangle of
cross-stitched Aida.

■ Cut the 3½x5-inch rectangle from the
cardboard and the batting.

■ Glue the batting to the cardboard, then
cover with the cross-stitched Aida fabric
(see Padded Shapes, page 166).

■ Glue the covered rectangle on the front
of the recipe box.

■ Glue rattail cord around the rectangle
where the padded shape meets the box.

(continued)

Recipe Box
(continued)

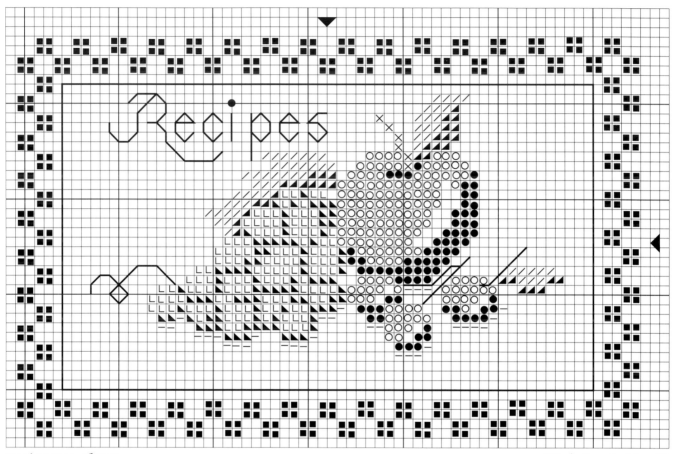

Recipe Box Chart

Stitch Count: 66 x 42

Floss: (Symbol indicates color on chart.)

Symbol	Color name	DMC #	Anchor #
○	Medium red	321	47
●	Dark red	814	45
/	Light green	504	875
◣	Dark green*	502	877
L	Light lavender	554	108
◤	Dark lavender	208	110
×	Brown*	898	359
	Blue*	3761	160
—	Light gray	415	398
■	Black	310	403

*Backstitch the stems with brown, letters with dark green, and inner border with blue, stitching over two squares.

For the Table

Coasters,
page 120

Bread Cover,
page 121

Place Mats,
page 122

Napkin Rings,
page 124

Coaster Chart   Stitch Count: 40 x 32

Coasters

1. Gather Materials

Aida fabric: 14 count, one 5-inch square
   each of dark green, dark brown, dark
   pink, and dark blue (MCG Textiles)
Coasters: 3 inch, acrylic (Fond
   Memories, Inc.)
Thick, white glue
Scissors

2. Stitch

Follow the cross-stitching instructions
given in Cross-Stitch Basics. Each coaster
is done in silhouette with only one color of
floss, a light tint to contrast with the dark
color of the fabric.

3. Finish

■ Use the foam insert that comes in the
coaster as a pattern. Center it over the
cross-stitched area of the Aida fabric, and
carefully cut away all excess Aida fabric.
■ Apply glue to entire back of foam insert.
Press onto back of cross-stitched Aida.
Allow glue to dry.
■ Insert foam-backed Aida into the
coaster.
■ Press plastic circle backing in the back of
the coaster to hold the Aida and foam in
place.

Floss: (Symbol is same for all colors;
coordinate color of floss with color of fabric)

Symbol	Color name	DMC#	Anchor #	Fabric color
V	Light green	504	875	Green
V	Light brown	842	376	Brown
V	Light pink	778	968	Dark pink
V	Light blue-gray	927	848	Dark blue
	Backstitch letters with same color as house.			

Bread Cover

1. Gather Materials

Bread cover: Premade, 18 inches square, Williamsburg blue, Royal Classic (Charles Craft, No. RC4850), *or* the following materials:

    Aida fabric: 14 count, Williamsburg blue, soft, washable fabric, 20 inches square

    Sewing machine or needle and thread

Scissors

Tapestry needle

2. Stitch

Follow the cross-stitching instructions given in Cross-Stitch Basics. The design is cross-stitched 2 inches in from the edge of the premade bread cover.

    If you cannot locate the specified bread cover, cross-stitch the design 3 inches in from the edge of a 20-inch square of Aida fabric and finish according to the following instructions.

3. Finish

Note: The premade bread cover requires no finishing. If you are making one, follow the instructions below.

■ After cross-stitching the design on Aida, cut 1 inch of fabric from all four sides, leaving an 18-inch square of cross-stitched fabric.

■ Stitch ½ inch inside all four sides of the fabric. Fringe all four sides to the stitching line by pulling out the horizontal threads.

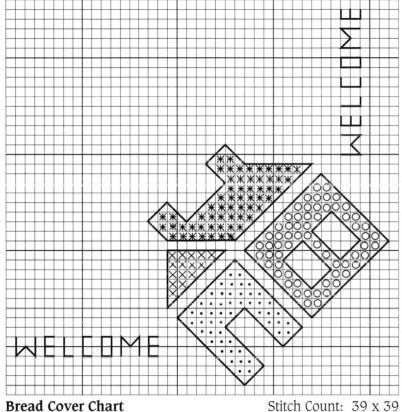

Bread Cover Chart Stitch Count: 39 x 39

Floss: (Symbol indicates color on chart.)

Symbol	Color name	DMC #	Anchor #
✕	Light brown	437	368
✳	Medium brown	839	944
	Dark blue*	823	150
•	Light pink	778	968
○	Dark pink	3733	76
	Black*	310	403

*Backstitch letters with dark blue and house with black.

Place Mats

1. Gather Materials

Aida fabric: 14 count, dark blue, 7½-inch square (for each place mat)
Premade place mats: Medium blue, quilted (see photo, page 119)
Satin ribbon: Pink, ⅛x20 inches
Scissors
Tapestry needle
Iron
Sewing machine or needle and thread
Fabric glue (optional)

2. Stitch

Follow the cross-stitching instructions given in Cross-Stitch Basics.

3. Finish

After cross-stitching the design on Aida, cut off 1 inch of the fabric from all four sides, leaving a 5½-inch square of cross-stitched fabric.

■ Fold back the Aida fabric ½ inch on all four sides of the cross-stitched design. Press the folds with an iron to crease. Hem the top edge.

■ Trim excess Aida fabric away at the corners, cutting at a 45-degree angle.

■ Sew the cross-stitched Aida fabric to the premade place mat, stitching along the sides and bottom to form a pocket.

■ Sew or glue ribbon on the sides and bottom of the pocket.

■ Repeat for each place mat.

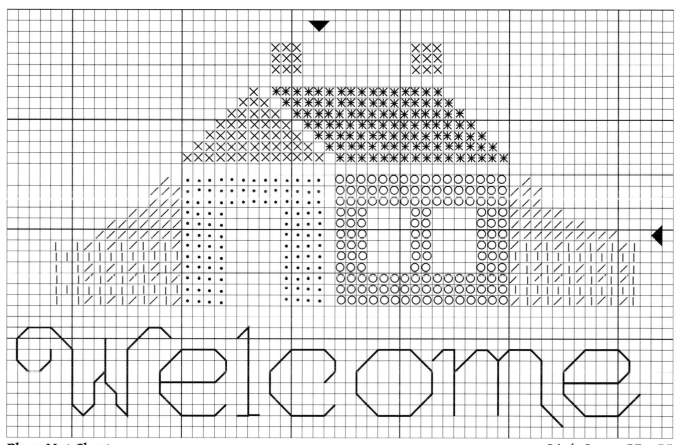

Place Mat Chart

Stitch Count: 57 x 35

Floss: (Symbol indicates color on chart.)

Symbol	Color name	DMC #	Anchor #
✳	Medium brown	839	944
✕	Light brown	437	368
╱	Medium green	368	261
│	White*	Snow white	1
•	Light pink	776	968
○	Medium pink	3733	76
	*Backstitch letters with white.		

Napkin Rings

1. Gather Materials

Aida fabric: 14 count, dark blue, 6x8 inches (for each napkin ring)
Thick, white glue
Scissors
Tapestry needle
Iron

2. Stitch

Follow the cross-stitching instructions given in Cross-Stitch Basics.

3. Finish

■ After cross-stitching the design on Aida, cut off 1 inch of fabric from all four sides, leaving a 4x6-inch rectangle of cross-stitched fabric.

■ Fold back fabric at the top and bottom of the design until the edges of the fabric meet in the center. Press the folds with an iron to crease. The napkin ring should now be 2 inches wide and 6 inches long.

■ Unfold the fabric, and apply an even coat of glue to the back of each flap; smooth flaps firmly back into place and allow to dry. As an alternative to gluing, you can stitch the two flaps together.

■ Bring the two ends of the napkin ring together, with raw ends pointing in. Glue or stitch the ends together with about a ½-inch overlap; pin together while glue dries.

■ Repeat for each napkin ring.

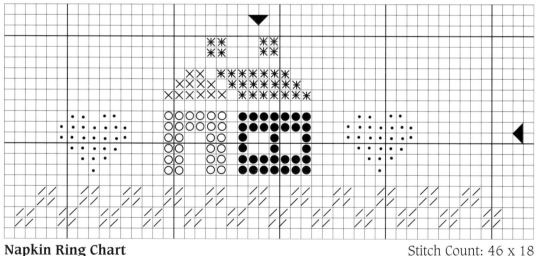

Napkin Ring Chart   Stitch Count: 46 x 18

Floss: (Symbol indicates color on chart.)

Symbol	Color name	DMC #	Anchor #
✳	Medium brown	839	944
•	Light pink	778	968
○	Medium pink	3733	76
●	Dark pink	3731	77
╱	Medium green	368	261
✕	Beige	437	368

Tissue Box
Cover,
page 129

Light Switch
Cover,
page 126

Banded Basket,
page 127

Hand Towel,
page 128

Light Switch Cover

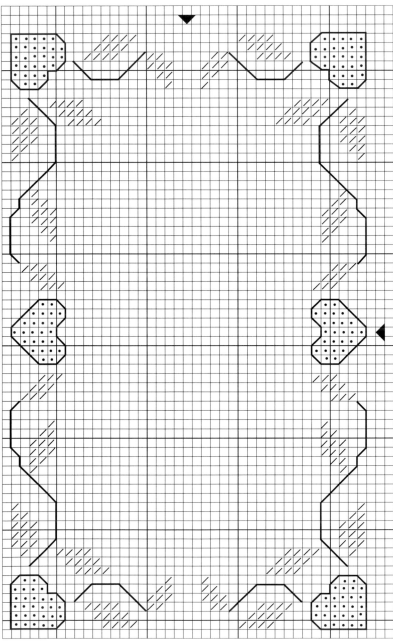

Light Switch Cover Chart

Stitch Count: 39 x 65

1. Gather Materials

Aida fabric: 14 count, white, 7x9 inches
Acrylic Designer Switch Plate:
(Fond Memories, Inc.)
Poster board: Lightweight, white,
3x5 inches
Thick, white glue
Scissor
Tapestry needle

2. Stitch

Follow the cross-stitching instructions
given in Cross-Stitch Basics.

3. Finish

General assembly instructions are given in
the switch plate package. The following are
additional instructions for this project.

■ After cross-stitching is complete, use the
foam that comes with the switch plate as a
pattern to cut the poster board and the Aida
fabric to size. Center the foam over the
Aida, trace around it, and cut just inside the
mark. Be sure to cut out the center
rectangle for the on/off switch to pass
through; this is easy to do if you make a
hole with your scissors near the middle of
the center rectangle, then cut out to the
corners and along the edges of the
rectangle. Repeat with foam and poster
board.

Floss: (Symbol indicates color on chart.)

Symbol	Color name	DMC #	Anchor #
/	Light green	912	205
	Dark green*	910	229
•	Light pink	957	52
	Dark pink*	956	54

*Backstitch the vines with dark green and
around the hearts with dark pink.

■ Use the poster board as the backing for the cross-stitched Aida. Put an even coat of thick, white glue on the poster board; press the back of the cross-stitched Aida firmly onto the poster board. Allow glue to dry.

■ Place the cross-stitched side down into the acrylic switch plate. Put the foam in next. Use a sharp-pointed tool (like an ice pick or large nail) to poke holes in the fabric and poster board where the screws will attach the plate to the wall. Install with the screws that come with the switch plate.

Banded Basket

1. Gather Materials

Ribband: 14 count, white Aida, pink scalloped edge, 1¾x30 inches, *or* the following materials:

    Aida fabric: 14 count, white, 4x30 inches

    Ribbon: ¼x60 inches, *or* lace: ½x60 inches

Basket: 5 inches wide, 9 inches long, 4½ inches high

Tapestry needle

Iron

Washable fabric glue

Scissors

Sewing machine or needle and thread (optional)

2. Stitch

Follow the cross-stitching instructions given in Cross-Stitch Basics.

    If you cannot locate Ribband, cross-stitch the design on the Aida fabric and finish according to the following instructions.

3. Finish

Measurements assume a basket of the dimensions given in materials list; adjust as necessary for smaller or larger baskets.

■ After cross-stitching the design on Ribband, cut 1 inch off each end. If cross-stitching on Aida, cut off 1 inch of fabric around all four edges.

■ Fold back Ribband or Aida ½ inch on each end of the cross-stitched design. Press the folds with an iron to crease.

■ Hemstitch the folded ends or glue them in place. To glue, unfold the fabric, and apply an even coat of glue to each flap; smooth the flaps firmly into place and allow glue to dry.

■ Apply fabric glue to the entire back of the cross-stitched Ribband or Aida; press firmly in place on the basket just beneath the top rim. Start and end on the back of the basket.

■ If using Aida, glue ribbon or lace over the raw edges of the fabric at the top and bottom of the band (where the Ribband has scalloped edges), starting and ending on the back of the basket.

Floss: (symbol indicates color on chart.)			
Symbol	Color name	DMC #	Anchor #
•	Light pink	957	52
	Dark Pink*	956	54
	Medium green	912	205
/	Dark green*	910	229

*Backstitch vines with dark green and hearts with dark pink.

Banded Basket Chart (Repeat design as needed to cover the entire band.)

Stitch Count: 6 x length needed to fit basket

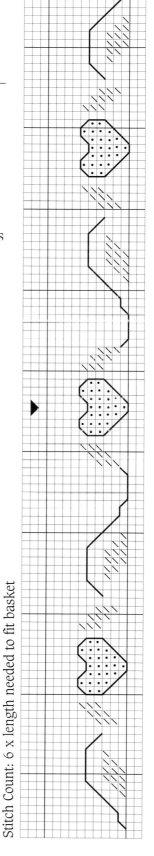

Hand Towel

1. Gather Materials

Towel: Premade, 11x18 inches, with 2-inch-wide even-weave fabric insert woven in horizontally (Charles Craft, No. 10300W), *or* plain towel without even-weave band and the following materials:

>   **Aida fabric:** 14 count, white, 5x14 inches, *or* Ribband: 2x14 inches
>   **Washable lace:** White, ½x32 inches (if not using Ribband)
>   **Iron**
>   **Sewing machine or needle and thread (optional)**

Scissors
Tapestry needle

2. Stitch

Cross-stitch the design on the band of the premade towel. Follow the cross-stitching instructions given in Cross-Stitch Basics.

If you cannot locate a towel premade with an even-weave insert, cross-stitch the design on Aida fabric or Ribband and finish according to the instructions.

3. Finish

Note: The premade towel requires no finishing. If you are adding a cross-stitched panel to a plain towel, use the following instructions.

■ After cross-stitching the design on Aida, cut off 1 inch of the fabric from all four sides, leaving a 3x12-inch piece of cross-stitched fabric. If using Ribband, cut 1 inch off only the ends.
■ Fold back the Aida fabric ½ inch on all four sides of the cross-stitched design. Press the folds with an iron to crease. If using Ribband, fold back only the ends and press.
■ Trim excess Aida fabric away at the corners, cutting at a 45-degree angle.
■ Unfold the fabric, and apply an even coat of glue to each flap; smooth the flaps firmly into place and allow glue to dry. As an alternative to gluing, you can hemstitch the flaps in place with a needle and thread.
■ Sew the cross-stitched Aida or Ribband to the towel, centering it about 1½ inches above the bottom edge of the towel.
■ Stitch the lace along the raw edges of the Aida strip (where Ribband has scalloped edges.)

Floss: (Symbol indicates color on chart.)

Symbol	Color name	DMC #	Anchor #
•	Light pink	957	52
	Dark pink*	956	54
/	Medium green	912	205
	Dark green*	910	229

*Backstitch vines with dark green and the hearts with dark pink.

Hand Towel Chart (Repeat design as needed to extend across the towel.)
Stitch Count: 6 x 105

Tissue Box Cover

1. Gather Materials

Tissue holder: 14 count, white (Crafters Pride), *or* the cutting diagrams, right, and the following materials:
>   **Aida fabric:** 14 count, white, 1 piece 5¼ x 21¾ inches, 2 pieces 5¼ x 8¾ inches
>   **Lace:** White, ½x20 inches
>   **Elastic:** ⅛x10 inches
>   **Sewing machine**

Scissors

Tapestry needle

2. Stitch

Follow the cross-stitching instructions given in Cross-Stitch Basics. Start cross-stitching the bottom of the design about ½ inch up from the bottom of the premade tissue holder.

If you cannot locate the specified tissue holder, cross-stitch the design ¾ inch up from the bottom edge of one of the 5¼ x 8¾-inch pieces of Aida.

3. Finish

Note: The premade tissue holder requires no finishing. If you are making one, use the following instructions.

■ Place the cross-stitched piece (face down) on top of the 5¼ x 21¾-inch piece of Aida near one end (right sides together). Stitch the two pieces together on one side allowing a ¼-inch seam (see Diagram A). (Zigzag all seams to prevent fraying.)

■ Continuing with right sides together, pin and stitch the bottom edge and side of the cross-stitched piece of Aida to the 5¼ x 21¾-inch piece of Aida (see Diagram B).

■ Sew the remaining 5¼ x 8¾-inch piece of Aida to the 5¼ x 21¾-inch piece of Aida in the same manner (see Diagram C).

■ Stitch the lace just inside the top edge of the holder.

■ Zigzag stitch the elastic 2 inches from the top of the wrong side of the Aida fabric, stretching 2½ inches of elastic to the 5-inch width of each side of the holder.

■ Turn tissue holder right-side out and fill with a boutique-size box of tissues.

(continued)

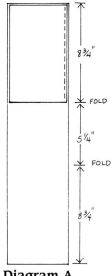

Diagram A

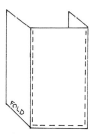

Diagram B

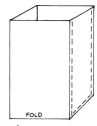

Diagram C

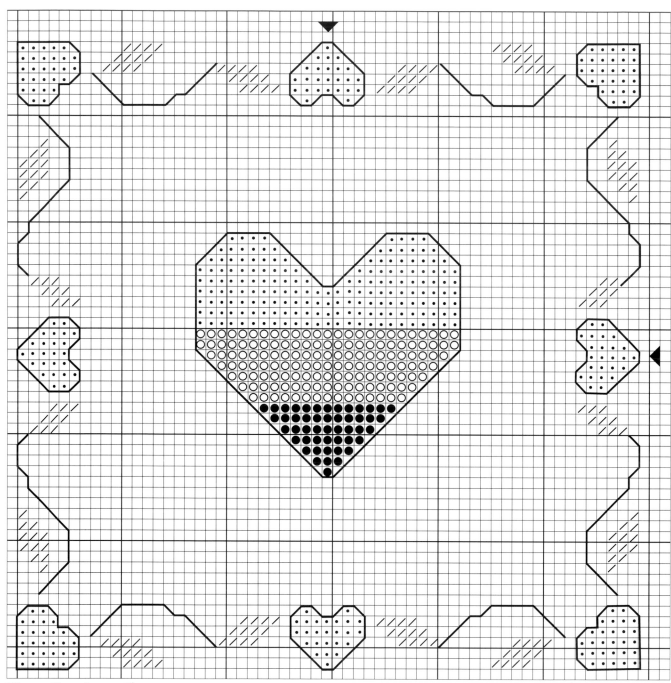

Tissue Box Cover Chart

Floss: (Symbol indicates color on chart.)

Stitch Count: 59 x 59

Symbol	Color name	DMC #	Anchor #
/	Light green	912	205
·	Pale pink	818	49
○	Light pink	776	50
●	Medium pink*	957	52
	Dark Pink	956	54
	Dark green*	910	229

*Backstitch vines with dark green (two strands) and around hearts with dark pink (one strand).

Classic Sampling

Home Sweet Home Sampler,
page 136

Kitchen Sampler,
page 134

Bandbox,
page 132

Bandbox

1. Gather Materials

Aida fabric: 14 count, Fiddler's Cloth, 8x10 inches
Wooden bandbox: Oval, approximately 5 x 7½ x 3 inches
Cardboard: Heavyweight, 12 inches square
Poster board: Lightweight, 5x8 inches
Batting: 5x8 inches
Rattail cord: Dark green, 40 inches
Thick, white glue
Scissors
Tracing paper
Tapestry needle

2. Stitch

Follow the cross-stitching instructions given in Cross-Stitch Basics. Personalize the box using the block alphabet on page 169.

3. Finish

Finishing instructions for covering padded shapes are given in General Project Instructions. The following are additional instructions for this project.

■ Trace the top of the box onto tracing paper. Draw another line about 1 inch outside the first to create a second oval. Center the pattern for the second oval over the cross-stitched fabric, and cut off excess fabric.

■ Cover cardboard oval with batting, then with cross-stitched fabric.

■ Glue covered oval on the top of the box.

■ Glue rattail cord in a double row where padded shape meets the box top.

Floss: (Symbol indicates color on chart.)

Symbol	Color name	DMC #	Anchor #
✕	Brown	838	380
•	Light peach	353	6
○	Dark peach*	352	10
V	Light blue	932	921
▼	Dark blue	930	922
╱	Light green	502	877
◢	Dark green*	500	879

*Backstitch lettering and its border with dark green and date with dark peach.

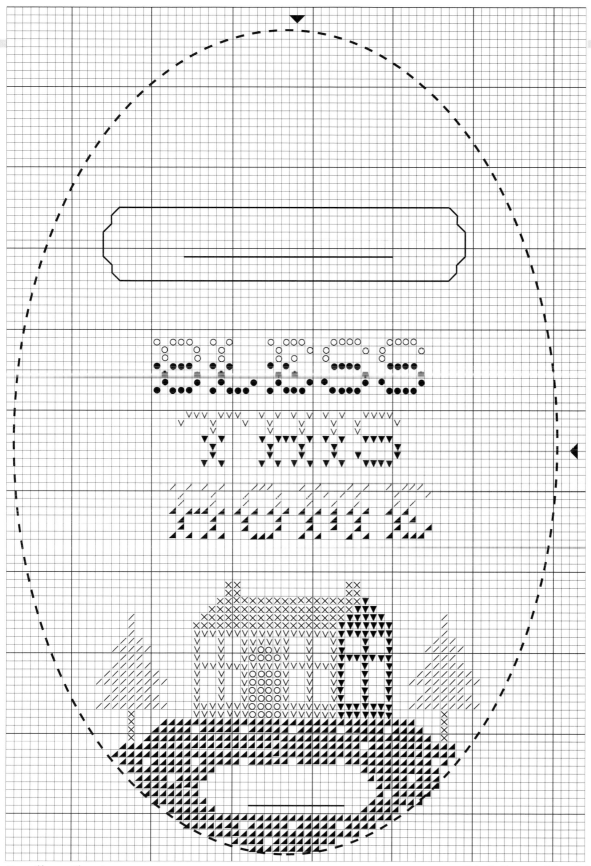

Bandbox Chart

Stitch Count: 48 x 81

133

Kitchen Sampler

1. Gather Materials

Floba fabric: 18 count, 14½x17½ inches
Frame: 14½x17½ inches with 12½x15½-
  inch opening
Mat: Coral, 7½x10½-inch opening
Mounting board: With peel and stick
  surface, 12½x15½ inches
Thick, white glue or needle and thread
Tapestry needle
Scissors
Iron

2. Stitch

Follow the cross-stitching instructions
given in Cross-Stitch Basics for cross-
stitching over two threads. Start cross-
stitching 4 inches up from the bottom of
the fabric.

3. Finish

■ Cut 1 inch off all sides of the fabric
leaving a 12½x15½-inch rectangle of
fabric.
■ Mount the fabric on the mounting board.
■ Place the mat and the mounted fabric
into the frame.

Floss: (Symbol indicates color on chart.)

Symbol	Color name	DMC #	Anchor #
✕	Brown	839	944
•	Light peach	353	8
○	Medium peach	352	10
●	Dark peach*	351	11
V	Light blue	932	920
▼	Dark blue	930	922
╱	Light green	504	875
◢	Dark green	502	877
	*Backstitch bottom heart with dark peach.		

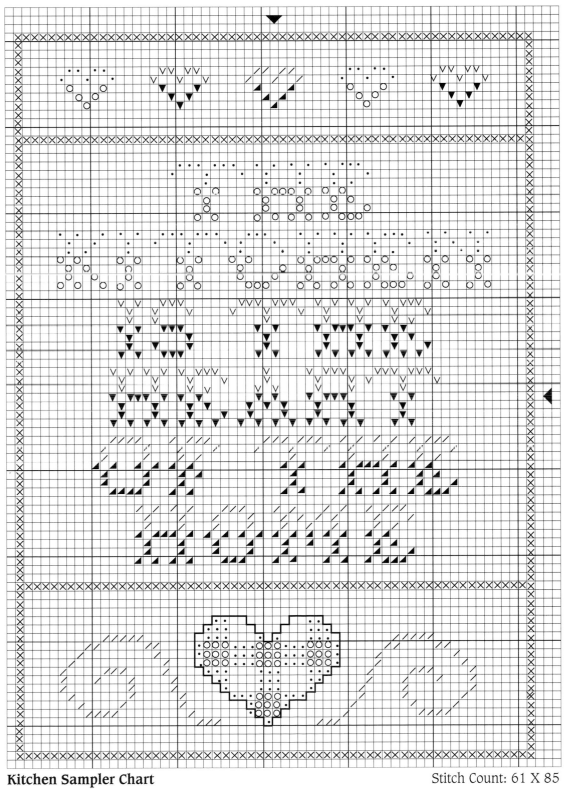

Kitchen Sampler Chart

Stitch Count: 61 X 85

Home Sweet Home Sampler

1. Gather Materials

Floba fabric: 14 count, 14x20 inches
Rattail cord: Brown, 24 inches
Tapestry needle
Thick, white glue
Scissors

2. Stitch

Follow the cross-stitching instructions given in Cross-Stitch Basics for cross-stitching over two threads. Personalize the sampler using the block alphabet on page 169.

3. Finish

■ Cut 1 inch off all sides of the fabric to leave a 12x18-inch rectangle of fabric.
■ Fringe the bottom edge ½ inch by pulling out the horizontal threads.
■ Fold back the fabric ½ inch on the two sides of the design; press folds with an iron to crease.
■ Unfold the fabric, and apply an even coat of glue to each flap; smooth flaps firmly back into place and allow to dry. As an alternative to gluing, you can hemstitch the flaps in place.
■ Wrap 1 inch of the top of the Aida fabric over the ribbon and dowel, and glue to the back of the Aida to form a casing. Allow glue to dry.
■ Tie the rattail cord to each end of the dowel for a hanger.

Floss: (Symbol indicates color on chart.)

Symbol	Color name	DMC #	Anchor #
✕	Brown	839	944
•	Light peach	352	10
○	Dark peach	351	11
V	Light blue	932	920
▼	Dark blue	930	922
╱	Light green	504	875
	Dark green*	502	877

*Backstitch lettering with dark green.

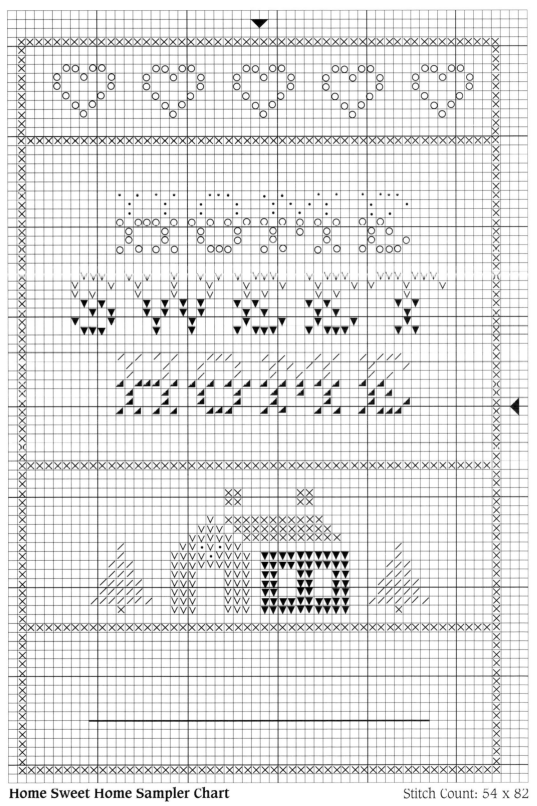

Home Sweet Home Sampler Chart

Stitch Count: 54 x 82

Gifts to Wear

❖ ❖ ❖

Warm the hearts of women and children

alike with an intriguing piece of beaded

jewelry or a simple T-shirt cleverly

embellished with a cross-stitch design.

You can choose from a host of fashionable

accessories on the following pages.

House Socks,
page 142

Floral Heart T-Shirt,
page 140

Flower Basket T-Shirt,
page 141

Checked Heart Socks,
page 143

Floral Heart T-Shirt

1. Gather Materials

Waste canvas: 8.5 count, 8 inches square
T-shirt: Pink
Rescue tape: 32 inches *or* needle
and thread
Pearls: ⅛ inch diameter *or* Tulip Color
Point™ Paint, snow white (#30)
Scissors
Tweezers
Sponge or spray bottle and water
Embroidery needle

2. Stitch

Attach the waste canvas to the front of the T-shirt following the instructions given in Cross-Stitch Basics for using waste canvas. Cross-stitch the heart design about 1½ inches below the neckline on the center front of the T-shirt.

Add pearls after other cross-stitching is complete, following the instructions for stitching with beads given in Cross-Stitch Basics. Or, put a drop of Tulip Color Point™ Paint in the center of each flower. This gives the pearl-like appearance shown in the photograph on page 139.

3. Finish

■ When all cross-stitching is complete (except for adding pearls), remove the basting or, if you used Rescue tape, pull up the edges of the waste canvas.
■ Trim the excess waste canvas close to the cross-stitched design, taking care not to clip the T-shirt or the stitches.
■ Dampen the waste canvas remaining on the T-shirt, using a sponge or spray bottle and water, to make the fibers pliable.
■ Use tweezers to pull the horizontal and vertical waste canvas threads, one at a time, from beneath the stitching.
■ Stitch on pearls where indicated on the chart.

Floral Heart Chart   Stitch Count: 40 x 33

Floss: (Symbol indicates color on chart.)

Symbol	Color name	DMC #	Anchor #
•	Dark pink	3731	77
/	Dark green	502	877
	White	Snow white	1

Flower Basket
T-Shirt

1. Gather Materials

Waste canvas: 8.5 count, 8 inches square
T-shirt: Pink
Rescue tape: 32 inches *or* needle
   and thread
Scissors
Tweezers
Sponge or spray bottle and water
Embroidery needle

2. Stitch

Attach the waste canvas to the front of the T-shirt following the instructions given in Cross-Stitch Basics for using waste canvas. Cross-stitch the flower design about 2 inches below the neckline on the center front of the T-shirt using three strands of floss.

3. Finish

■ When all cross-stitching is complete, remove the basting or, if you used Rescue tape, pull up the edges of the waste canvas.
■ Trim the excess waste canvas close to the cross-stitched design, taking care not to clip the T-shirt or the stitches.
■ Dampen the waste canvas remaining on the T-shirt, using a sponge or spray bottle and water, to make the fibers pliable.
■ Use tweezers to pull the horizontal and vertical waste canvas threads, one at a time, from beneath the stitching.

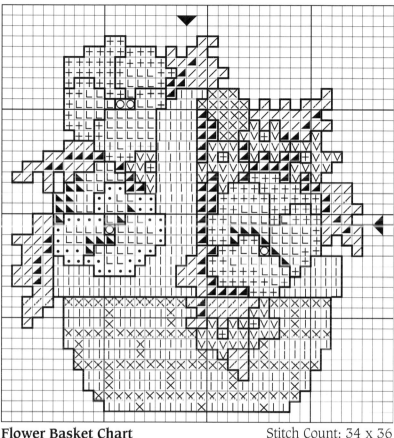

Flower Basket Chart   Stitch Count: 34 x 36

Floss: (Symbol indicates color on chart.)

Symbol	Color name	DMC #	Anchor #
+	Light yellow	3078	292
○	Light orange	741	316
V	Medium blue	931	921
╱	Light green	504	875
◣	Medium green	502	877
I	Light brown	437	372
✕	Dark brown	434	375
L	Light lavender	554	108
◥	Medium lavender	553	98
•	White	Snow white	1
	Black*	310	403
	*Backstitch with two strands of black.		

House Socks

1. Gather Materials

Waste canvas: 14 count, 2x12 inches
Socks: Khaki, with cuff
Rescue tape: 8 inches, cut in half
 lengthwise, *or* needle and thread
Scissors
Tweezers
Sponge or spray bottle and water
Embroidery needle

2. Stitch

Turn the sock inside out. Attach the waste canvas to the top edge of the sock following the instructions given in Cross-Stitch Basics for using waste canvas. (If using Rescue tape, cut tape in half lengthwise so that it doesn't interfere with the stitching area of the waste canvas.) Turn the sock upside down and cross-stitch the design right side up about ¼ inch from the top of the sock. (Be sure the sock is inside out while cross-stitching.) When done, turn right side out and turn down cuff.

3. Finish

■ When the cross-stitching is complete, remove the basting or, if you used Rescue tape, pull up the edges of the waste canvas.
■ Trim the excess waste canvas close to the cross-stitched design, taking care not to clip the socks or the stitches. Discard the removed canvas.
■ Dampen the waste canvas remaining on the socks, using a sponge or spray bottle and water, to make the fibers pliable.
■ Use tweezers to pull the horizontal and vertical waste canvas threads, one at a time, from beneath the stitching.

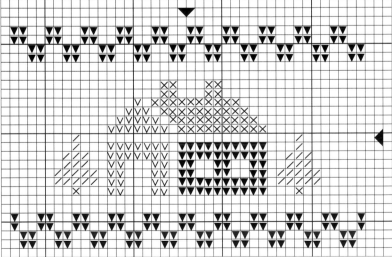

House Socks Chart
(Continue check design around sock cuff.)

Stitch Count: sock cuff circumference x 25

Floss: (Symbol indicates color on chart.)

Symbol	Color name	DMC #	Anchor #
╱	Light green	522	859
V	Light blue	794	120
▼	Dark blue	931	921
✕	Brown	3790	898

Checked Heart Socks

1. Gather Materials

Waste canvas: 14 count, 2x10 inches
  (or enough to cover top of each sock)
Socks: Pink, with cuff
Rescue tape: 10 inches, cut in half
  lengthwise, *or* needle and thread
Scissors
Tweezers
Sponge or spray bottle and water
Embroidery needle

2. Stitch

Turn the sock inside out. Attach the waste canvas to the top edge of the sock following the instructions given in Cross-Stitch Basics for using waste canvas. (If using Rescue tape, cut tape in half lengthwise so that it doesn't interfere with the stitching area of the waste canvas.) Turn the sock upside down and cross-stitch the design right side up about ¼ inch from the top of the sock. (Be sure the sock is inside out while cross-stitching.) When done, turn right side out and turn down cuff.

3. Finish

■ When the cross-stitching is complete, remove the basting or, if you used Rescue tape, pull up the edges of the waste canvas.
■ Trim the excess waste canvas close to the cross-stitched design, taking care not to clip the socks or the stitches. Discard the removed canvas.
■ Dampen the waste canvas remaining on the socks, using a sponge or spray bottle water, to make the fibers pliable.
■ Use tweezers to pull the horizontal and vertical waste canvas threads, one at a time, from beneath the stitching.

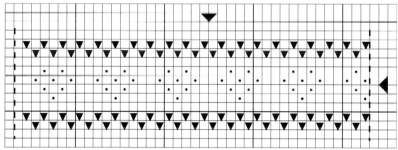

Checked Heart Socks Chart
(Continue design around sock cuff.)

Stitch Count: sock cuff
circumference x 10

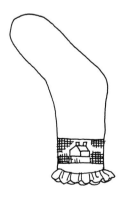

Floss: (Symbol indicates color on chart)

Symbol	Color name	DMC #	Anchor #
▼	Medium blue	932	920
•	Dark peach	353	9

Fashion Statement

Quilt Floral Necklace,
page 149

Folk Heart
Necklace,
page 150

Fleur-de-lis Pin,
page 146

Tulip Pin,
page 145

Fan Barrette,
page 147

Fan Earrings,
page 148

Tulip Pin

1. Gather Materials

Perforated paper: 14 count, black,
  4 inches square (Yarn Tree Designs, Inc.)
Felt or decorative paper: Black, 2 inches
  square
Pin back: ¾ inches long
Glass seed beads: Light pink, medium
  pink, dark pink, light green, dark green,
  light blue, and black (Mill Hill Glass Seed
  Beads, Gay Bowles Sales)
Thick, white glue
Glue gun or strong glue for metal
Quilting needle: No. 11
Scissors

2. Stitch

Follow the instructions for stitching with
beads given in Cross-Stitch Basics. Use a
single strand of floss in the same color as
the bead. If desired, the design can be
cross-stitched without beads using two
strands of floss and making full cross-
stitches.

3. Finish

■ Carefully cut off the excess paper around
the design, cutting through the first row of
holes just beyond the stitching (the first
holes without thread in them).
■ Use the pattern, right, to cut a felt or
decorative paper backing for the design. It
should be about ¹⁄₁₆ inch smaller than the
perforated paper. Spread an even layer of
white glue on the backing, and put it on
the back of the cross-stitched perforated
paper.
■ Glue the pin back centered in the back of
the pin using a glue gun or other strong
glue.

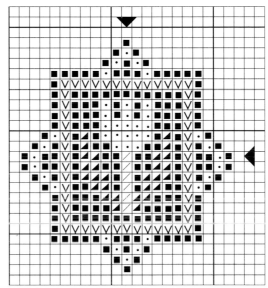

Tulip Pin Chart   Stitch Count: 21 x 23

Floss: (Symbol indicates color of floss and bead on chart.)

Symbol	Color name	DMC #	Anchor #	Bead #
•	Medium pink	776	74	2005
/	Light green	954	204	525
◢	Dark green	911	205	167
V	Light blue	813	160	2007
■	Black	310	403	81

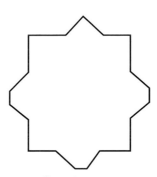

Tulip Pin
Full-Size Pattern

Fleur-de-lis Pin

1. Gather Materials

Perforated paper: 14 count, gold,
  5 inches square (Yarn Tree Designs, Inc.)
Felt or decorative paper: Black,
  3 inches square
Pin back: 1¼ inches long
Glass seed beads: Pink, light green, light
  blue, lavender, and black (Mill Hill Glass
  Seed Beads, Gay Bowles Sales)

Thick, white glue
Glue gun or strong glue for metal
Quilting needle: No. 11
Scissors

2. Stitch

Follow the instructions for stitching with
beads given in Cross-Stitch Basics. Use a
single strand of floss in the same color as
the bead. If desired, the design can be
cross-stitched without beads using two
strands of floss and making full cross-
stitches.

3. Finish

■ Carefully cut off the excess paper around
the design, cutting through the first row of
holes just beyond the stitching (the first
holes without thread in them).
■ Use the pattern, below, to cut a felt or
decorative paper backing for the design. It
should be about ¹⁄₁₆ inch smaller than the
perforated paper. Spread an even layer of
white glue on the backing, and put it on
the back of the stitched perforated paper.
■ Glue the pin back centered in the back of
the pin using a glue gun or other strong
glue.

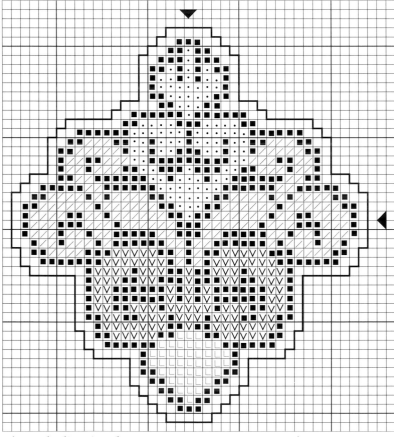

Fleur-de-lis Pin Chart Stitch Count: 37 x 41

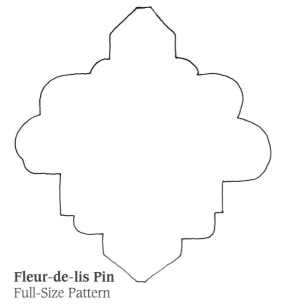

Fleur-de-lis Pin
Full-Size Pattern

Floss: (Symbol indicates color of floss and bead on chart.)

Symbol	Color name	DMC #	Anchor #	Bead #
•	Pink	776	74	2005
/	Light green	954	204	525
V	Light blue	809	117	146
L	Lavender	210	108	2009
■	Black	310	403	0081

Fan Barrette

1. Gather Materials

Perforated paper: 14 count, gold, 3x6 inches (Yarn Tree Designs, Inc.)
Felt or decorative paper: Black, 2x4½ inches
Barrette back: 3 inches long
Glass seed beads: Light pink, dark pink, light green, purple, and black (Mill Hill Glass Seed Beads, Gay Bowles Sales)
Thick, white glue
Glue gun or strong glue for metal
Quilting needle: No. 11
Scissors

2. Stitch

Follow the instructions for stitching with beads given in Cross-Stitch Basics. Use a single strand of floss in the same color as the bead. If desired, design can be cross stitched without beads using two strands of floss and making full cross-stitches.

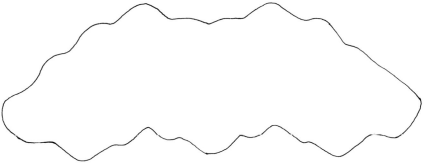

Fan Barrette
Full-Size Pattern

3. Finish

■ Carefully cut off the excess paper around the design, cutting through the first row of holes just beyond the stitching (the first holes without thread in them).
■ Use the pattern, above, to cut a felt or decorative paper backing for the design. It should be about ⅟₁₆ inch smaller than the perforated paper. Spread an even layer of white glue on the backing, and put it on the back of the stitched perforated paper.
■ Glue the barrette back centered in of the back using a glue gun or other strong glue.

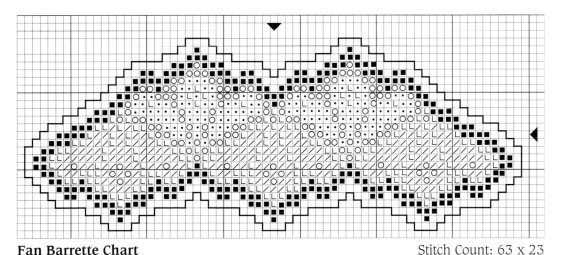

Fan Barrette Chart

Stitch Count: 63 x 23

Floss: (Symbol indicates color of floss and bead on chart.)

Symbol	Color name	DMC #	Anchor #	Bead #
•	Light pink	3733	76	2004
○	Dark pink	3350	65	968
╱	Light green	954	204	525
L	Purple	3746	119	252
■	Black	310	403	2014

Fan Earrings

1. Gather Materials

Perforated paper: 14 count, gold, two pieces each 2x3 inches (Yarn Tree Designs, Inc.)

Felt or decorative paper: Black, 2x4½ inches

Earring backs: Post type for pierced earrings; clip type for nonpierced earrings

Glass seed beads: Dark pink, light green, purple, and black (Mill Hill Glass Seed Beads, Gay Bowles Sales)

Other beads: Pearl teardrops, white 6; tubes, ¼ inch long, black, 6

Thick, white glue

Glue gun or strong glue for metal

Quilting needle: No. 11

Scissors

2. Stitch

Follow the instructions for stitching with beads given in Cross-Stitch Basics. Use a single strand of floss in the same color as

the bead. If desired, design can be cross-stitched without beads using two strands of floss and making full cross-stitches.

3. Finish

■ Carefully cut off the excess paper around the design, cutting through the first row of holes just beyond the stitching (the first holes without thread in them).

■ Thread needle with a black thread about 12 inches long; double the thread and knot it. Thread on a black tube bead, a dark pink seed bead, a pearl teardrop bead, and another pink seed bead; run the needle back through the pearl teardrop, center pink, and black tube beads. Repeat stringing beads five times. Attach a string of beads to the end of a curved part of the fan by running the needle up through the back of the perforated paper, over one hole, and back to the back of the paper; knot on the back. Repeat until all six strings of beads have been attached to the earrings (see photo, page 144).

■ Use the pattern, below, to cut a felt or decorative paper backing for the design. It should be about ¹⁄₁₆ inch smaller than the perforated paper. Poke the post backs through the felt or paper backing about ¼ inch down from the small end (top); if using clip earring backs, apply them with strong glue after the felt or paper backing has been glued on the back of the beading. Spread an even layer of glue on the felt or paper backing and on the earring back. Press the backing onto the back of the stitched perforated paper.

■ Allow glue to dry.

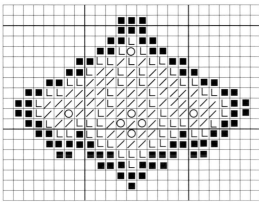

Fan Earring Chart   Stitch Count: 23 x 17

Fan Earrings
Full-Size Pattern

Floss: (Symbol indicates color of floss and bead on chart.)

Symbol	Color name	DMC #	Anchor #	Bead #
○	Dark pink	3350	65	968
/	Light green	954	204	525
L	Purple	3746	119	252
■	Black	310	403	2014

Quilt Floral Necklace

1. Gather Materials

Aida fabric: 14 count, Williamsburg blue,
4½ inches square
Stik 'N Puff: Two, 2¼ inches squares
(BANAR DESIGNS, Inc.), *or* pattern,
below, and the following materials:
   Cardboard: Heavyweight,
     2¼x4½ inches
   Batting: 2¼x4½ inches
   Thick, white glue
Backing fabric: 4½ inches square
(you can use Aida or cotton fabric in a
coordinating color)
Rattail cord: 60 inches
Wooden beads: Two, ½ inch long
(optional)
Glue gun or thick, white glue
Scissors
Tapestry needle

2. Stitch

Follow the cross-stitching instructions
given in Cross-Stitch Basics. Note: This
design is cross-stitched on the diagonal,
with one corner of the design in the center
of each side of the Aida, about ¾ inch from
the edge of the fabric.

3. Finish

Finishing instructions for covering padded
shapes are given in General Project
Instructions. The following are additional
instructions for this project.
- If you do not have Stik 'N Puff squares,
use the inner square of the pattern, right;
cut the shape from cardboard and batting.
- Cover a Stik 'N Puff (or cardboard
layered with batting) with the cross-
stitched Aida fabric.
- Cover the second Stik 'N Puff (or
cardboard layered with batting) with the
backing fabric.

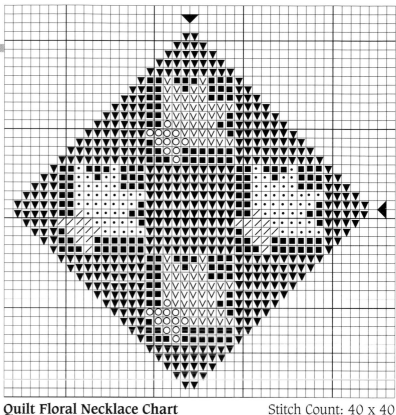

Quilt Floral Necklace Chart　　　　Stitch Count: 40 x 40

Floss: (Symbol indicates color on chart.)

Symbol	Color name	DMC #	Anchor #
•	Pink	224	893
V	Light blue	3756	158
▼	Medium blue	931	921
/	Green	501	877
○	Gold	437	368
■	Black	310	403

**Quilt Floral
Necklace**
Full-Size Stitched
Fabric Pattern
(use inner square
for cardboard and
batting)

- Cut a 42-inch length of rattail for the
hanging cord. Lay the center of the cord
across the back of the Aida-covered
square, about ½ inch from the top of the
design.
- Glue the two padded squares back to
back.
- Glue the remaining rattail cord around
the edges where the padded shapes meet,
starting at the bottom and running the
rattail around the squares two times. Cut
off any excess cord.
- Tie a simple knot in each side of the
hanging cord about 1 inch from the
necklace. Thread a bead on each cord, and
tie another knot to keep the bead in place.
- Tie the two ends of the cord together in a
simple knot. Try necklace on to check the
length; if necessary, adjust the knot. Cut
off excess length.

Folk Heart Necklace

1. Gather Materials

Aida fabric: 14 count, ivory,
3½ inches square
Stik 'N Puff: Two, 2¼ inches square
(BANAR DESIGNS, Inc.), *or* pattern on
page 149 and the following materials:
    Cardboard: Heavyweight,
      2¼x4½ inches
    Batting: 2¼x4½ inches
  Thick, white glue
Backing fabric: 3½ inches square (you
can use Aida or natural muslin)
Rattail cord: 38 inches
Glue gun or thick, white glue
Scissors
Tapestry needle

2. Stitch

Follow the cross-stitching instructions
given in Cross-Stitch Basics.

3. Finish

Finishing instructions for covering padded
shapes are given in General Project
Instructions. The following are additional
instructions for this project.
■ If you do not have Stik 'N Puff squares,
use the inner square of the pattern on page
149; cut the shape from the cardboard and
the batting.
■ Cut a 2-inch length of rattail cord for the
loop at the top of the necklace. Center and
glue the ends of this cord on the back of
the Aida-covered square at the top of the
design.
■ Glue the two squares back to back,
making sure the loop extends out between
the squares.

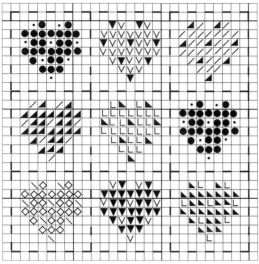

Folk Heart Necklace Chart
Stitch Count: 27 x 27

Floss: (Symbol indicates color on chart.)

Symbol	Color name	DMC #	Anchor #
•	Light pink	224	893
●	Medium pink	223	895
V	Light blue	3756	158
▼	Medium blue	931	921
╱	Light green	504	875
◢	Dark green	501	877
L	Light lavender	3042	870
◣	Dark lavender	3041	871
╲	Light yellow	3078	292
◇	Gold	437	368
	Gray*	318	235

*Backstitching with gray is done to
resemble the running stitch in quilting.

■ Run the remaining rattail cord through
the loop. Tie the ends of the cord together
in a simple knot. Try necklace on to check
the length; if necessary, adjust the knot.
Cut off excess length.

Minitote,
page 154

Tote Bag,
page 152

Tote Bag

1. Gather Materials

Waste canvas: 8.5 count, 11x13 inches
Canvas tote bag: 13 inches square
Rescue tape: 48 inches *or* needle
  and thread
Scissors
Tweezers
Sponge or spray bottle and water
Embroidery needle

2. Stitch

Attach the waste canvas to the center front of the tote bag following the instructions given in Cross-Stitch Basics for cross-stitching using waste canvas. To make cross-stitching easier, you may want to remove one of the side seams of the tote bag; restitch the seam when you are finished cross-stitching.

3. Finish

■ When all cross-stitching is complete, remove the basting or, if you used Rescue tape, pull up the edges of the waste canvas.

■ Trim the excess waste canvas close to the cross-stitched design, taking care not to clip the tote bag or the stitches.

■ Dampen the waste canvas remaining on the tote bag, using a sponge or spray bottle and water, to make the fibers pliable.

■ Use a tweezers to pull the horizontal and vertical waste canvas threads, one at a time, from beneath the stitching.

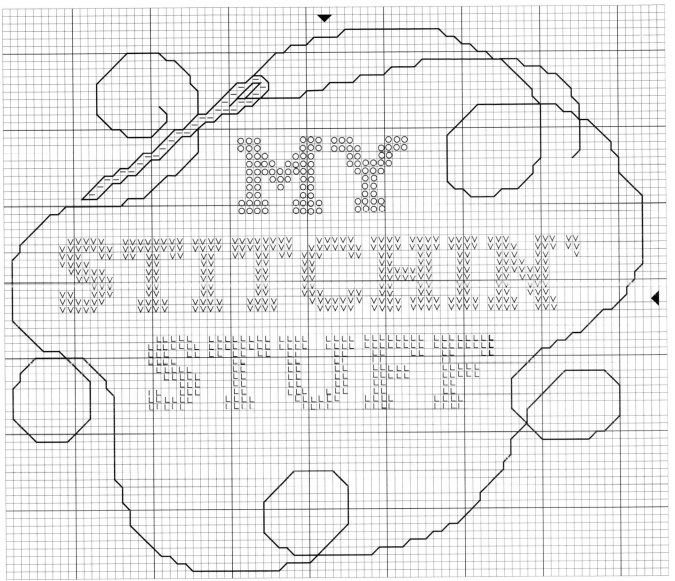

Tote Bag Chart

Stitch Count: 91 x 71

Floss: (Symbol indicates color on chart.)

Symbol	Color name	DMC #	Anchor #
○	Medium pink	957	52
V	Medium blue	798	146
L	Dark lavender	553	98
—	Gray	415	398
	Black*	310	403
	Green*	319	218

*Backstitch the thread with medium green
and the needle with black.

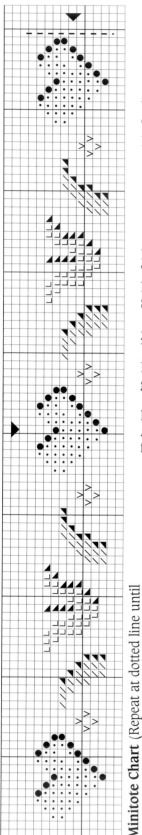

Minitote

1. Gather Materials

Tote bag: Straw, 7x3x6 inches
Ribband: 14 count, ecru Aida fabric with scalloped edge, 1x22 inches, *or* the following materials:
    Aida fabric: 14 count, ecru, 2x22 inches:
    Lace: ¼x40 inches
    Fabric glue
Ribbon: Satin, ¼x20 inches
Tapestry needle
Iron
Scissors

2. Stitch

Follow the cross-stitching instructions given in Cross-Stitch Basics.

If you cannot locate the specified Ribband, cross-stitch the design on the Aida fabric and finish according to the following directions.

3. Finish

Measurements assume a tote of the dimensions given above; adjust as necessary for smaller or larger totes.

■ After cross-stitching the design on Ribband, cut ½ inch off the ends. If stitching is done on Aida, cut off ½ inch of the fabric on all four sides.

■ Fold back the Ribband or Aida ½ inch on each end of the cross-stitched design. Press the folds with an iron to crease.

■ Glue the folded ends or hemstitch them in place. To glue, unfold the fabric flaps, and apply an even coat of glue to each flap; smooth the flaps firmly into place and allow to dry.

■ Apply fabric glue to the entire back of the cross-stitched Ribband or Aida; press firmly in place on the tote near the center. Start and end on the back of the tote.

■ If using Aida, glue ribbon or lace over the raw edges of the fabric at the top and bottom of the band (where the Ribband has scalloped edges), starting and ending on the back of the tote.

■ Apply fabric glue to the back of the satin ribbon. Slide it just under the bottom edge of the Ribband or lace, starting and ending on the back of the tote.

Floss: (Symbol indicates color on chart.)

Symbol	Color name	DMC #	Anchor #
·	Light pink	957	52
●	Medium pink	956	54
>	Medium blue	799	145
◣	Light lavender	554	108
◢	Medium lavender	553	98
╱	Light green	368	214
◥	Medium green	367	217

For the Kids

Halloween T-Shirt,
page 159

Heart Socks,
page 156

Fourth of July T-Shirt,
page 158

Kitty Socks,
page 157

Heart Socks

1. Gather Materials

Waste canvas: 14 count, 2x10 inches
  (or enough to cover top of each sock)
Socks: White, with cuff (lace edge
  optional)
Rescue tape: 10 inches, cut in half
  lengthwise, *or* needle and thread
Scissors
Tweezers
Sponge or spray bottle and water
Embroidery needle

2. Stitch

Turn the sock inside out. Attach the waste canvas to the top edge of the sock following the instructions given in Cross-Stitch Basics for using waste canvas. (If using Rescue tape, cut tape in half lengthwise so that it doesn't interfere with the stitching area of the waste canvas.)

Turn the sock upside down and cross-stitch the design right side up about ¼ inch from the top of the sock. (Be sure the sock is inside out while cross-stitching.) When done, turn right side out and turn down cuff.

3. Finish

■ When the cross-stitching is complete, remove the basting or, if you used Rescue tape, pull up the edges of the waste canvas.
■ Trim off the excess waste canvas close to the cross-stitched design, taking care not to clip the socks or the stitches.
■ Dampen the waste canvas remaining on the socks, using a sponge or spray bottle and water, to make the fibers pliable.
■ Use tweezers to pull the horizontal and vertial waste canvas threads, one at a time, from beneath the stitching.

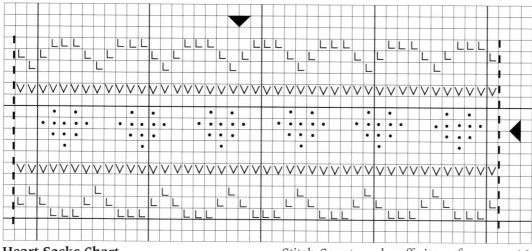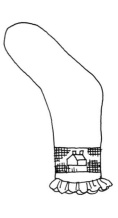

Heart Socks Chart
(Continue design around sock cuff.)

Stitch Count: sock cuff circumference x 16

Floss: (Symbol indicates color on chart.)

Symbol	Color name	DMC #	Anchor #
L	Light lavender	554	108
V	Medium blue	799	145
•	Medium pink	957	52

Kitty Socks

1. Gather Materials

Waste canvas: 14 count, 2x6 inches
Socks: Blue, with cuff
Rescue tape: 8 inches, cut in half
  lengthwise, *or* needle and thread
Scissors
Tweezers
Sponge or spray bottle and water
Embroidery needle

2. Stitch

Turn the sock inside out. Attach the waste canvas to the top edge of the sock following the instructions given in Cross-Stitch Basics for using waste canvas. (If using Rescue tape, cut tape in half lengthwise so that it doesn't interfere with the stitching area of the waste canvas.) Turn the sock upside down and cross-stitch the design right side up about ¼ inch from the top of the sock. (Be sure the sock is inside out while cross-stitching.) When done, turn right side out and turn down cuff.

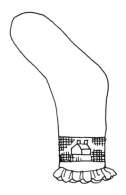

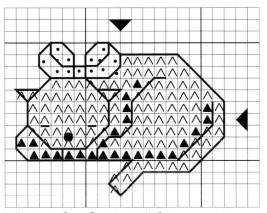

Kitty Socks Chart   Stitch Count: 18 x 13

Floss: (Symbol indicates color on chart.)

Symbol	Color name	DMC #	Anchor #
∧	Light Peach	754	6
•	Pink	776	50
▲	Dark Peach	353	8
	Medium gray*	414	235
	Black*	310	403

*Backstitch with medium gray. Nose is a French knot done in black.

3. Finish

■ When the cross-stitching is complete, remove the basting or, if you used Rescue tape, pull up the edges of the waste canvas.

■ Trim the excess waste canvas close to the cross-stitched design, taking care not to clip the socks or the stitches.

■ Dampen the waste canvas remaining on the socks, using a sponge or spray bottle and water, to make the fibers pliable.

■ Use tweezers to pull the horizontal and vertical waste canvas threads, one at a time, from beneath the stitching.

Fourth of July T-Shirt Chart

Stitch Count: 27 x 45

Fourth of July T-Shirt

1. Gather Materials

Waste canvas: 8.5 count, 8 inches square
T-shirt: Child or adult size
Rescue tape: 32 inches or needle
  and thread
Star-shaped sequins (optional)
Washable fabric glue (optional)
Scissors
Tweezers
Sponge or spray bottle and water
Embroidery needle

2. Stitch

Attach the waste canvas to the front of the T-shirt following the instructions given in Cross-Stitch Basics for using waste canvas. Cross-stitch the cat design with the hat about 2 inches below the neckline of the shirt. All cross-stitches are done using six strands of floss.

3. Finish

■ When all cross-stitching is complete, remove the basting or, if you used Rescue tape, pull up the edges of the waste canvas.
■ Trim the excess waste canvas close to the cross-stitched design, taking care not to clip the T-shirt or the stitches.
■ Dampen the waste canvas remaining on the T-shirt, using a sponge or spray bottle and water, to make the fibers pliable.
■ Use tweezers to pull the horizontal and vertical waste canvas threads, one at a time, from beneath the stitching.
■ Glue on star-shaped sequins, if desired.

Floss: (Symbol indicates color on chart.)

Symbol	Color name	DMC #	Anchor #
○	Red	321	47
V	Blue	824	148
+	Metallic gold	282	4640
—	Gray	415	398
■	Black*	310	403

*Backstitch with black using two strands.

Halloween T-Shirt

1. Gather Materials

Waste canvas: 8.5 count, 5 inches square
T-shirt or sweatshirt: Child or adult size, orange or white
Rescue tape: 20 inches *or* needle and thread
Scissors
Tweezers
Sponge or spray bottle and water
Embroidery needle

2. Stitch

Attach the waste canvas to the left front of the T-shirt following the instructions given in Cross-Stitch Basics for using waste canvas. Cross-stitch the witch design with the top about 2 inches below the neckline and halfway between the center of the shirt and the armhole. Use all six strands for all cross-stitching.

3. Finish

■ When all cross-stitching is complete, remove the basting or, if you used Rescue tape, pull up the edges of the waste canvas.
■ Trim the excess waste canvas close to the cross-stitched design, taking care not to clip the T-shirt or the stitches.
■ Dampen the waste canvas remaining on the T-shirt, using a sponge or spray bottle and water, to make the fibers pliable.
■ Use tweezers to pull the horizontal and vertical waste canvas threads, one at a time, from beneath the stitching.

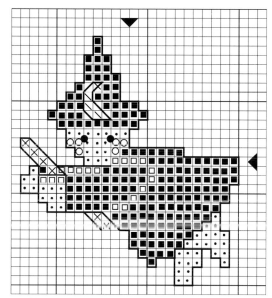

Halloween T-Shirt Chart
Stitch Count: 24 x 27

Floss: (Symbol indicates color on chart.)

Symbol	Color name	DMC #	Anchor #
·	Flesh	940	6
○	Pink	957	52
■	Black*	310	403
□	Dark gray	414	235
\	Yellow	3078	300
×	Brown	433	371
	*Backstitch with black.		

■ Make the broom straw using 20 strands of yellow floss, each 4 inches long. Fold the floss in half; wrap an 8-inch length of yellow floss around the folded strands about ¼ inch down from the fold. Tie securely, and trim off excess. Stitch the folded end to the shirt at the end of the broom handle.

Santa T-Shirt,
page 161

Christmas Cat Sweater,
page 162

Santa T-Shirt

1. Gather Materials

Waste canvas: 8.5 count, 6 inches square
T-shirt: Red
Pompons: White, 1 inch; red, ½ inch
Rescue tape: 24 inches *or* needle
  and thread
Scissors
Tweezers
Sponge or spray bottle and water
Embroidery needle
Thread or washable fabric glue

2. Stitch

Attach the waste canvas to the front of the T-shirt following the instructions given in Cross-Stitch Basics for using waste canvas. Cross-stitch the Santa design about 1 inch below the neckline on the center front of the T-shirt.

3. Finish

■ When the cross stitching is complete, remove the basting or, if you used Rescue tape, pull up the edges of the waste canvas.

■ Trim the excess waste canvas close to the cross-stitched design, taking care not to clip the T-shirt or the stitches.

■ Dampen the waste canvas remaining on the T-shirt, using a sponge or spray bottle and water, to make the fibers pliable.

■ Use tweezers to pull the horizontal and vertical waste canvas threads, one at a time, from beneath the stitching.

■ Stitch or glue the white and red pompons in place at the top of the hat and just above the mustache (see photo, page 160).

■ To make the beard, cut 28 lengths of white floss (use all six strands), each 7 inches long. Thread the needle with one length (six strands) at a time; run needle

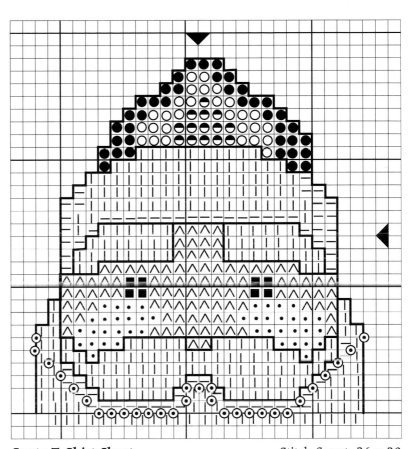

Santa T-Shirt Chart   Stitch Count: 26 x 29

Floss: (Symbol indicates color on chart.)

Symbol	Color name	DMC #	Anchor #
○	Medium red	321	19
●	Dark red	816	22
·	Light pink	3326	50
◐	Dark pink	3716	51
∧	Light peach	754	6
■	Black	310	403
│	White	Snow white	1
—	Gray	415	398
⊙	Attach floss for beard at these points.		

through the fabric from the front where indicated on the chart; pull 3½ inches of floss through. Tie a simple knot on the back; bring the remainder of the floss back to the front of the fabric through the same hole; remove needle. Repeat until all 28 lengths of floss have been stitched on.

Christmas Cat Sweater

1. Gather Materials

Waste canvas: 8.5 count, 5 inches square
Sweater: Red or white
Beads: Red, ⅛ inch diameter, 6
Rescue tape: 20 inches *or* needle
  and thread
Scissors
Tweezers
Sponge or spray bottle and water
Embroidery needle

2. Stitch

Attach the waste canvas to the front of the sweater following the instructions given in Cross-Stitch Basics for using waste canvas. Cross-stitch the cat design with the top about 1 inch below the neckline of the sweater; use three strands of floss. Remove waste canvas before stitching on beads with red floss; if you cannot find red beads, make French knots with red floss where beads are indicated on the chart.

3. Finish

■ When all cross-stitching is complete, remove the basting or, if you used Rescue tape, pull up the edges of the waste canvas.
■ Trim the excess waste canvas close to the cross-stitched design, taking care not to clip the sweater or the stitches.

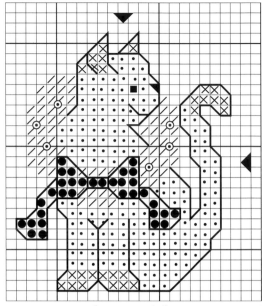

Cat Sweater Chart   Stitch Count: 20 x 25

Floss: (Symbol indicates color on chart.)

Symbol	Color name	DMC #	Anchor #
•	Beige	437	369
✕	Medium brown	435	370
╱	Green	910	228
●	Metallic gold	282	4640
■	Black*	310	403
⊙	Large red beads or Red floss	321	47

*Backstitch cat and bow with two strands of black floss.

■ Dampen the waste canvas remaining on the sweater, using a sponge or spray bottle with plain water, to make the fibers pliable.
■ Use a tweezer to pull the horizontal and vertical waste canvas threads, one at a time, from beneath the stitching.
■ Stitch on the red beads as indicated on the chart.

Photo Albums

Materials
(See individual projects for amounts.)

Photo album: Ring-binder type
Fabric
Batting: 1 inch thick
Ruler
Felt-tip pen
Scissors
Thick, white glue
Poster board
Fabric-covered, padded shape
   (generally with stitching on it)
Lace, ribbon, rattail cord, or other
   decoration, if desired

Directions (See diagrams for clarification.)

Note: Remove album pages while covering album; replace pages when glue is dry.

1. Place opened album on wrong side of fabric. Trace around the album with felt-tip pen. Add 1¾ inches all the way around, and cut out.

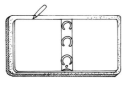

2. Place opened album on 1-inch-thick batting. Trace around it with felt-tip pen. Cut out on line.

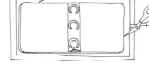

3. Cut two strips of fabric 1½ inches wide and ½ inch longer than the backbone of the album. Fold each end under ¼ inch and press folds to crease. Run thin line of glue down groove on each side of metal spine in center of album. Glue fabric strips down as close to metal spine as possible, or pry metal up slightly and slip fabric under edges. Then glue down remaining edges of fabric strip.

4. Lay fabric wrong side up; place batting in center. Place album on top of batting. Apply thin layer of glue to all corners of album cover. Pull fabric up and into glue at corners.

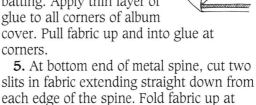

5. At bottom end of metal spine, cut two slits in fabric extending straight down from each edge of the spine. Fold fabric up at end of metal spine, and trim fabric to fit just under spine. Apply thin layer of glue along bottom edge of album. Fold fabric up into glue and smooth. At metal spine, fold fabric up into glue and, if possible, slip under the end of the metal; otherwise, fold fabric under and glue at end of spine.

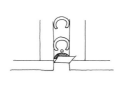

6. Repeat the previous step at the top edge of the album (turn the top edge of the album toward you to make it easier to work with). Pull the fabric taut so there are no wrinkles.

7. Apply glue to the side edges of the album. Fold fabric up into the glue.

8. Apply thin layer of glue ¼ inch inside edges of album on top of just-glued fabric. Press lace into glue, starting and ending at center bottom of album.

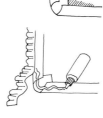

9. To round corners, pinch extra lace between your fingers and press into glue.

10. If you want ribbon ties on album, glue two or three lengths of ribbon to the center of each side of the album cover.

(continued)

Photo
Albums
(continued)

11. Measure length and width of the inside covers of album. Cut two pieces of lightweight poster board this size. Cut two fabric pieces 1 inch larger than this size. Lay fabric pieces wrong side up; place poster board pieces on top. Put glue around all edges of poster board; fold fabric up into glue, mitering corners (fold in from corners first, then sides). Put glue over the just-glued fabric. Turn over and place the poster board pieces, fabric sides up, on the inside of the album covers, covering the edges of any lace or ribbon already glued down.

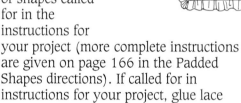

12. Make any covered shape or shapes called for in the instructions for your project (more complete instructions are given on page 166 in the Padded Shapes directions). If called for in instructions for your project, glue lace around the back of the shape.

13. Glue covered shape(s) to the front of the album. If a more finished look is desired, add rattail cord to cover where the shape meets the album cover or the lace meets the edges.

Photo Frames

Materials
(See individual projects for amounts.)

Heavyweight cardboard: Such as 300-pound illustration board or precut photo frame with easel
Fabric: Cotton or cotton/polyester blend
Batting
Trims: Rattail cord, lace, or other as specified in project
Tracing paper
Thick, white glue

Scissors
Pencil
Felt-tip pen
Crafts knife, utility knife, or single-edged razor blade

Directions (See diagrams for clarification.)

Note: Cover front, back, and easel of frame separately, then assemble.

1. Cut heavyweight cardboard using pattern specified in project; be sure to trace and cut both the inner and outer lines.

2. Hold the frame front up to a light, and place the cross-stitched fabric in front of it. Center the cross-stitched design over the cardboard, making sure no cross-stitching extends off the edge or into the center opening. Hold the fabric tightly in place on the cardboard and turn over on table with cross-stitched design down, cardboard up; be sure the cardboard is aligned evenly with the threads of the fabric. With a pencil, trace around the cardboard on the fabric, both outside the edge and inside the center opening.

3. Remove cardboard, and trim fabric about ½ inch beyond the pencil marks (larger rectangle). Miter corners (see illustration), cutting almost to pencil-marked corners.

4. Clip fabric every ½ inch on inside of center opening (in a sunburst shape) to within ⅛ inch of the pencil mark.

5. Place cardboard frame front on cotton batting and trace the shape, inside and out, with a felt-tip pen. Cut out and glue shape onto cardboard.

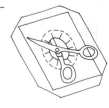

6. Place fabric on table, cross-stitched (or right) side down. Turn batting-covered cardboard upside down on fabric, lining it up with pencil marks on fabric.

7. Spread glue around outer edges of cardboard. Wrap fabric around outer cardboard edges and press into glue. Pull fabric as you work to keep it from wrinkling. Put a spot of glue in each corner, and work the corner fabric into it until it sticks, forming a neatly rounded corner; it will be moldable like clay. Press any loose threads into the glue.

8. Spread glue around the center opening. Pull fabric tightly into the opening, and press into glue. Pull any loose threads of fabric around to the back of the cardboard, and press into glue. 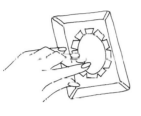 Push and mold the fabric into the wet glue to make smooth edges (wash your hands several times as you work so fabric doesn't stick to your fingers). Look at the front of the fabric to make sure cuts in the fabric are not showing; if they are, keep pulling the fabric onto the back. If you want to add lace, do it at this time; spread glue near the edge of the back of the covered frame front, and lay lace around edge, pinching extra lace at the corners. Start and end lace at center bottom, overlapping ends slightly.

9. Cover the backing cardboard with fabric of your choice, coordinating with your cross-stitched design. Cut the backing cardboard, using the same pattern as the front, but not cutting out the center opening. Cut the fabric as you did in steps 2 and 3, and glue as in step 7, using a thin coat of glue so it won't soak through the fabric.

10. Spread a thin layer of glue on the front side of the backing cardboard that you have just covered (this area will show through the opening in the frame). Glue on a piece of fabric that is slightly larger than the opening.

11. Cut strips of cardboard ½ inch wide and as long as the two sides and bottom of your frame. Glue the strips in place on the cardboard backing to form a holder for your picture (see illustration). If you wish, these strips also can be covered with fabric, at least on the outside edges and ends that will show.

12. When both front and back of frame are dry, glue them together, applying glue only to the cardboard strips around the edges.

13. Cut the easel out of cardboard (see pattern). Score (cut slightly) horizontally with knife about 1 inch from the top (flat end). Place the easel on a scrap of fabric, and trace around it with pencil. Cut out a shape ½ inch larger than this tracing. Miter the corners of the fabric, and clip up to the points on the easel (see illustration). Glue the fabric to the cardboard easel. Trace the easel shape with pencil onto another scrap of fabric, and cut it about ¼ inch smaller than the pencil mark. Glue this fabric to the back of the fabric-covered easel.

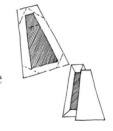

14. Glue easel to back of frame, positioning as shown in illustration.

15. Add trims such as rattail cord around edges, if desired. Use the cord to cover the spacer strips if you didn't cover them with fabric. If you used lace, glue the cord where the stitched fabric meets the lace. Start gluing at bottom corner, and glue to very edge of top of frame so opening at top remains. Slide photo in position.

Padded Shapes

Materials
(See individual projects for amounts.)

**Stik 'N Puffs precut, padded shapes
with peel-and-stick backs**
(or heavyweight cardboard, such as
300-pound illustration board, and
batting to create your own)
Fabric: Cotton or cotton/polyester blend
Trims: Rattail cord, lace, or other as
specified in project
Tracing paper
Thick, white glue
Scissors
Pencil
Felt-tip pen

Directions (See diagrams for clarification.)

1. If you are not using a Stik 'N Puff
shape, cut heavyweight cardboard and
batting using inner line of pattern or the
size specified in project.

2. Pin the fabric pattern to the fabric, and
cut out on the outer line; if no pattern is
given, cut the fabric ¾ inch larger than the
size specified in the project. If the fabric is
cross-stitched, hold the pattern and fabric
up to a light or window to center the cross-
stitching in the pattern area.

3. Remove liner paper from Stik 'N Puff
to expose sticky backing. If not using Stik
'N Puff, glue batting to cardboard.

4. Lay fabric on
table, right side
down. Place Stik 'N
Puff or batting-
covered cardboard
over fabric,
cardboard side up. If not using a Stik 'N

Wrong side
of fabric

Puff shape, run a line of glue around edge
of cardboard.

5. Press center of cardboard down to
compress padding. Pull the fabric up
around the padding, and press it into the
adhesive on the
back of the
cardboard. Look
at the front of
the fabric-
covered shape; if
there are any

"points" showing on curved shapes, apply
a drop of glue to the cardboard in back of
the point, and work the fabric into the glue
until the area is smooth.

6. If using a square or rectangular shape,
pull fabric sides up into adhesive. Apply a
drop of glue to each corner, and smooth
the fabric into the glue to seal the fabric to
cardboard.

7. If the project calls for lace, run a line
of glue about ⅛ inch in from the edge of
the shape on
the fabric on
the back of the
cardboard.
Press the lace
into the glue,

pinching in extra at the corners to make an
attractive turn.

8. Glue the shape to an album or, for an
ornament, glue two shapes back-to-back
after adding a hanging cord at the top.
Glue rattail cord around the ornament, if
desired, to cover the area where the shapes
meet; start and end behind the hanger cord
(see illustration).

There are several alphabet styles provided on pages 168–171: use the alphabet specified in your project. Use the blank graph provided and a pencil to copy the letters for the name or date you want.

■ Backstitch lettering should have only one blank space between letters.
■ The script alphabet is designed so lowercase letters connect to each other.
■ Large block lettering should have two blank spaces between letters.
■ Experiment with the lettering you are using; you may want more or less space between the letters to heighten visual appeal.

Positioning Names and Dates

■ When you have the name or date as you want to stitch it, count the number of stitches in the width of the name; divide the total by two and mark the horizontal center on your graph.
■ Count the number of stitches in the height of the name; divide the total by two and mark the vertical center on your graph.
■ Count the area on your stitched piece available for personalizing, vertically and horizontally, and mark the center. Match the center of the personalizing area on the fabric with the center on the graph.
■ Cross-stitch the personalized name or date.

If you are cross-stitching a long name within a border, you may need to extend the border to make room for the entire name. Other options are to use a shortened form of the name, or initials.

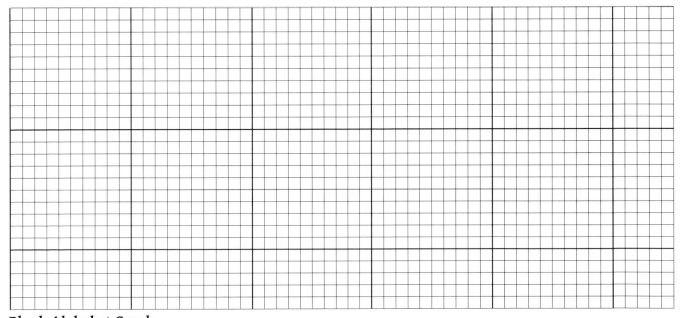

Blank Alphabet Graph

Script Alphabet

(Lowercase letters should connect.)

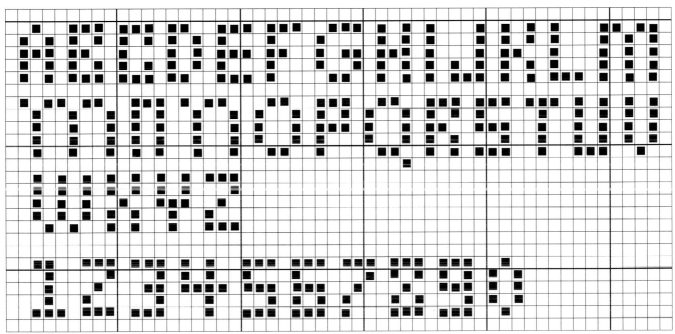

Block Alphabet (Leave one blank space between letters.)

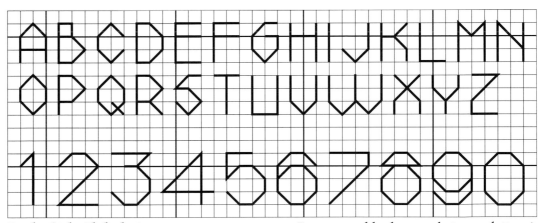

Backstitch Alphabet (Leave one blank space between letters.)

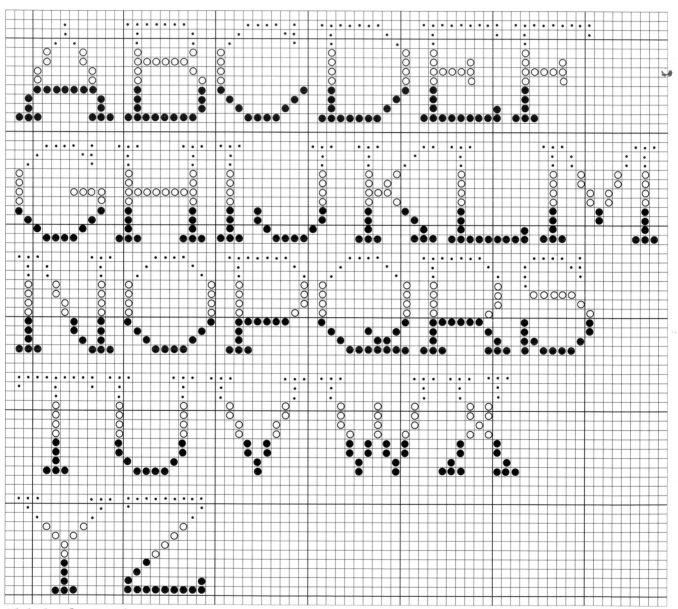

Alphabet for Cat Place Mat

(Use with Cat Place Mat on page 42.)

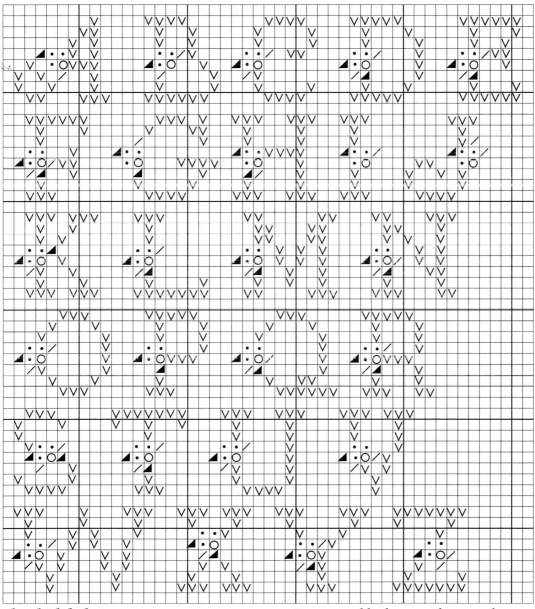

Floral Alphabet

(Leave two blank spaces between letters. Use with Tiny T-Shirt on page 67.)

Getting Started

Cross-stitching is needlework comprised mainly of X-shaped stitches that are formed by running threads through the holes in an even-weave fabric. This fabric—often white Aida, but available in many other types and colors—has threads evenly spaced vertically and horizontally to form a grid-like pattern. The "count" given for the fabric indicates how many stitches can be made per inch on the fabric; stitching on a fabric with a count that is different from what is indicated in the directions will result in a smaller or larger stitching area.

The cross-stitching technique has been simplified in this book to allow it to be done easily and quickly. Only full cross-stitches are used, along with backstitches, some French knots, and a few lazy daisy stitches for detailing.

On the project charts, each symbol represents one cross-stitch, and there is a different symbol for each color of floss (see diagram). A key for the symbols, showing the color names and floss numbers for both DMC and Susan Bates' Anchor floss, is also provided for each project.

The horizontal and vertical center of the design is marked with arrows on the chart. Find the center of your fabric by folding it in half in both directions and creasing the folds; unfold the fabric and use a straight pin or running stitch to mark these center folds. Stitch the design in the center of the fabric, comparing the position of the stitches on the graph to the position on the fabric; use the pins to correspond to the arrows on the graph.

When the project calls for perforated paper, do not fold the paper to find the center, but measure with a ruler instead; tie a thread through the holes on each side of center to mark it.

Tapestry needles are used in cross-stitch. They have blunt points to move through the holes in the fabric easily. Size 24 or 26 needles are best for cross-stitching on Aida fabric. Some stitchers like to hold their fabric tight and straight in a stitchery frame or embroidery hoop; while this is optional for very small projects, it does make cross-stitching easier on most projects.

 RED
BLACK

 CHART

 FABRIC

Stitching

Begin a project by cross-stitching the center of the design in the center of the fabric. The most successful method of cross-stitch is to pass your needle entirely down through the fabric before bringing it through to the front again. This allows you to keep the floss even and does not distort the fabric.

Unless otherwise indicated, do not knot the floss; hold about a ¼-inch tail of floss on the back of the fabric and cross-stitch over it with your first several cross-stitches to secure it. To end a thread, run the floss under several cross-stitches on the back to secure (see diagram). Cut off excess.

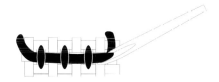

Most cross-stitching is done over one thread, passing the needle from the back up through one hole and back down through the next diagonal hole. To make stitching more prominent, some designs are cross-stitched over two threads, passing the needle up through one hole, skipping the next diagonal hole, and going back down through the second diagonal hole.

The following instructions detail the basic stitches used to make the projects in this book.

Cross-Stitch

■ Each individual cross-stitch is made up of two stitches that together form an X (see diagram). The bottom stitch is worked from lower left to upper right. The top stitch is worked from lower right to upper left.
■ Do a row of bottom stitches first, working from left to right (see diagram).

■ Complete the Xs by working the top stitches from right to left (see diagram).

Backstitch

■ Backstitching is shown on the cross-stitch charts in heavy black lines. It is used to define shapes by forming a continuous line around them or to create lettering.
■ Backstitches can go diagonally across one or two squares of fabric or around the perimeter of a fabric piece.
■ Do backstitching once the cross-stitching is complete.
■ The diagram illustrates backstitching. The needle came up at 1, went down at 2, came up at 3, went down at 4 (the same hole as 1), came up at 5, and went down at 6 (the same hole as 3). In this manner, you travel twice as far on the back of the fabric and reuse holes.

French Knot

■ Tie a knot in the end of the floss.
■ Bring the needle up from the back of the fabric, and pull the knot against the back of the fabric.

(continued)

Stitching

(continued)

■ Pull the floss taut. With the needle close to the hole it came up through, wrap the floss around the needle two or three times (see diagram).

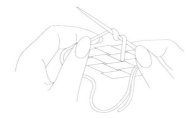

■ Hold the remaining floss firmly near the hole, and push the needle through a new hole next to the first hole. Continue to hold the floss taut with one hand while pushing the needle through the hole with the other (see diagram).

■ Pull the needle to the back of the fabric until the tail of the floss is on the back of the fabric; tie a knot on the back, and trim off excess.

Lazy Daisy Stitch

■ Bring the needle up from the back of the fabric.
■ Go back through the same hole, leaving a loop of floss on top of the fabric.
■ Bring the needle up through a nearby hole and position it inside the floss loop (see diagram). Pull the thread tight.

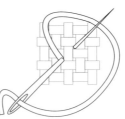

■ Pass the needle over the floss to the outside of the loop and take it back through the second hole (see diagram).

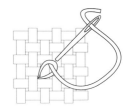

Using Perforated Paper

■ Cross-stitch on perforated paper just as you would on fabric, but be careful not to pull the floss too tightly or the paper may tear.
■ Whenever you are cutting out shapes cross-stitched on perforated paper, cut in the first empty hole outside the design; cutting through a stitched hole may cause the stitching to become loose or frayed.

Floss and Special Threads

■ Floss is composed of six strands. Cut an 18-inch length; take the desired number of strands for stitching in one hand, hold the rest in the other hand and pull it apart, letting the floss twist apart at the other end. Unless otherwise specified, cross-stitching is done with two strands; backstitching shapes is done with one strand, and lettering is backstitched with two strands.
■ Metallic floss may be used alone, but it has more impact when used with floss of a corresponding color. Use one strand of metallic gold and one strand of plain gold floss when metallic is specified on the color key.

Glass Beads

■ When stitching beads onto perforated paper, stitch all of them on the same angle using a half cross-stitch. Use only one strand of floss to attach the beads; for best results, match the color of the floss to the color of the beads.

- Use a No. 11 quilting needle or other sharp, thin embroidery needle.
- Bring the needle up through the fabric or paper, through a bead, and down through the next diagonal hole, completing a half cross-stitch. Each bead may seem loose until you stitch on the next one.
- Keep a few beads at a time in a small container such as a plastic lid. This makes them easier to thread onto the needle.
- Start and finish the floss just as you do in cross-stitching, passing it beneath several stitches on the back of the paper or fabric.

Using Waste Canvas

- Waste canvas is a stiff gridwork of threads used as a guide when stitching on fabrics that do not have an even weave. Follow these simple guidelines for using waste canvas.
- Cut waste canvas to the size specified in the project.
- To center the design on clothing, fold the garment in half lengthwise. Measure down this center fold to where you want the top of your design to be and mark the location with a pin.
- Measure to find the center of the canvas. Line the center of the canvas up with the center fold in the garment. Use the blue threads of the canvas to place the canvas squarely on the garment. Pin it in place so it is about ½ inch above where you want the design to start.
- Baste around all edges to hold the waste canvas firmly in place or use Rescue tape, a special double-sided tape especially for fabric.
- If desired, put the area in an embroidery hoop, making sure only one layer of the fabric is in the hoop.

- Cross-stitch the design using the large holes (not the small ones) where the threads intersect. When working on fabric, you can knot the floss on the back when starting and ending to make it more secure.
- After stitching, remove the basting thread or Rescue tape, and trim the canvas close to the edge of the stitching, being careful not to cut the fabric.
- Dampen the remaining canvas with a sponge or spray bottle of water to soften the fibers.
- Pull out the horizontal and vertical threads of the canvas, one at a time, using tweezers.

Finishing the Projects

- Complete instructions and patterns are included with each project, unless they are quite lengthy or are used for several projects. Those patterns and instructions are given in General Project Instructions beginning on page 163.
- Some projects, such as towels, hats, and bibs, are stitched on premade materials; manufacturers are listed with those materials. If you cannot find the materials at your local shop, a source list is given on page 176. As an alternative to premade materials, instructions are given for creating the same effect with readily available materials.

Look for the materials used in *100 Weekend Cross-Stitch Gifts* at your local needlework or craft shop. They were supplied by the following companies:

Acrylic bag tag/key ring, coasters, and light switch cover

Fond Memories, Inc.
One Terminal Way
Norwich, CT 06360
203-887-4789

Cardboard frames

Better Homes and Gardens® Book Club, which allowed us to reprint the patterns for those shapes.

Even-weave fabrics and waste canvas

Charles Craft
P.O. Box 1049
Laurinburg, NC 28352
(also supplied many of the premade items used)

MCG Textiles
5224 Bell Court
Chino, CA 91710

Fabric key case, scissors case, and Klostern pillow with plaid ruffle

Adam Originals
14568 S. 80th St.
Hastings, MN 55033
612-436-5615

Fun Mugs® (plastic mug for Dad)

Kelly's Crafts, Inc.
8170 Leeshore Dr.
Maineville, OH 45039
513-459-1113

Glass seed beads

Mill Hill Glass Seed Beads
c/o Gay Bowles Sales
P.O. Box 1060
Janesville, WI 53547
800-447-1332

Hat with Aida insert, royal lace guest towel, tissue holder, and vinyl Aida place mat

Crafter's Pride from Daniel Enterprises

Lucite house magnet

Wheatland Crafts
834 Scuffletown Rd.
Simpsonville, SC 29681
803-963-4920

Perforated paper

Yarn Tree Designs, Inc.
P.O. Box 724
Ames, IA 50010

Rescue tape

Seams Great
12710 Via Felino
Del Mar, CA 92014
619-755-7980

Ribband®

The Finish Line
P.O. Box 8515
Greenville, SC 29604
803-370-2166

(Ribband® used by permission of The Finish Line)

Stik 'N Puffs

BANAR DESIGNS, Inc.
P.O. Box 483
Fallbrook, CA 92028
619-728-0344

Waffle-weave (thermal) baby blanket

Designing Women, Unlimited
601 East 8th Street
El Dorado, AR 71730